PUNJAB POLITICS AND CONGRESS : 1947-66

PUNJAB POLITICS AND CONGRESS : 1947-66

Dr. Michael Khirdo Kinger

Commonwealth

Punjab Politics and Congress : 1947-66

Ist Edition : 2005
ISBN 81-7169-919-7

Published by :
Ajay Verma
For Commonwealth Publishers
4831/24, Prahlad Street,
Ansari Road, Darya Ganj,
New Delhi - 110002
Phone : 23272541, 23257835
Fax: 91-011-23257835
E-mail : campusbooks@hotmail.com

Laser Typesetting by :
Stylish Laser Typesetter
Delhi

Printed at :
Roshan Offset Printers
Delhi

Acknowledgements

During the course of the completion of this study, I was fortunate to have immense cooperation and inspiration from various sources and I take this opportunity to express my sincere gratitude to the concerned persons and agencies.

I am profoundly indebted to my esteemed teacher, learned guide and supervisor, **Dr. Param Bakhshish Singh**, Professor and Head, Department of Punjab Historical Studies, Punjabi University, Patiala, whose intelligent vision, constant supervision, learned guidance, pulsate enthusiasm and above all his most inspiring encouragement and humanitarian behaviour led me to complete this thesis in such an elegant form. Moreover being his student, I have learned to look at things in a much better way which in the long run will not only help me in being a better professional, but will also enrich my personal life. It has been my proud priviledge to work under such a caring teacher.

I am taking deep pleasure to record my sincere thanks to Dr. D.S. Dhillon, Professor & Head, Dr. Y.P. Bajaj, Former Professor, Dr. S.K. Gupta, Professor, all from Department of History, Punjabi University, Patiala, for their ever available guidance and personal interest throughout the course of the study.

I owe a special word of thanks to Dr. Devinder Verma, Dr. R.K. Ghai, and Dr. Navtej Singh, for their invaluable suggestions and encouragement.

I express my grateful thanks to Dr. K.L. Tuteja, Professor, Kurukshetra University, Kurukshetra, for his cooperation, which was abundantly extended to me.

Special thanks are due to my research colleagues and all other friends for their spontaneous help and constant words of encouragement.

Feelings cannot be expressed merely in words of thanks, which I owe to my parents and my family for their perennial encouragement, tolerance and patience, and their blessings, which enabled me to complete this study.

My grateful thanks are due to the staff of National Archives of India, New Delhi, Nehru Memorial Museum and Library, New Delhi, Jawaharlal Nehru University, New Delhi, Punjab State Archives, Patiala, Central State Library, Patiala, Punjab University, Chandigarh, Kurukshetra University, Kurukshetra, Punjabi University, Patiala and Department of Punjab Historical Studies, Punjabi University, Patiala, for allowing me to consult the concerned material and documents available with them.

I shall be failing in my duty if I do not express my gratitude to the authorities of the Indian Council of Historical Research, New Delhi, for providing me timely financial assistance to complete this work.

Dr. Michael Khirdo Kinger

Contents

List of Tables

List of Appendices

Abbreviations

- AICC - All India Congress Committee
- AISPC - All India States People's Conference
- BJS - Bhartiya Jan Sangh
- CKD - Chief Khalsa Diwan
- CPI - Communist Party of India
- IAR - Indian Annual Register
- ICHR - Indian Council of Historical Research
- INA - Indian National Army
- JVP - Jawaharlal Nehru, Vallabhbhai Patel and Pattabhi Sitaramayya
- KMPP - Kissan Mazdoor Praja Party
- NAI - National Archives of India, New Delhi
- NMML - Nehru Memorial Museum and Library, New Delhi
- NWFP - North-West Frontier Province
- n.d. - No date
- n.p. - No place
- PLA* - Punjab Legislative Assembly
- PPCC - Punjab Provincial Congress Committee
- PPP - Punjab Past and Present
- PSA - Punjab State Archives
- PSP - Praja Socialist Party
- PVS - Pepsu Vidhan Sabha
- RPI - Republican Party of India
- RSS - Rashtriya Swayamsewak Sangh

- SAD - Shiromani Akali Dal
- SGPC - Shiromani Gurdwara Prabandhak Committee
- SCF - Schedule Caste Federation
- SRC - States Reorganisation Commission
- WPIS - White Paper on Indian States

*Punjab Legislative Assembly (PLA) was later changed to Pepsu Vidhan Sabha (PVS).

1

Introduction

Every Society has developed the scientific knowledge and technical know-how according to its needs. Its level attained might have not been high. Pre-British Indian Society, which had been existing for centuries, was, therefore, not without any technological expertise. It lived by agriculture and handicrafts, which presupposed such sciences as astronomy, agronomy, mathematics and mechanics. Indian society in those days also possessed the science of medicine. Since the society stood at a low level of economic development, the amount of scientific knowledge, it had attained and accumulated was relatively small. The Indian people had done pioneering work in sciences such as mathematics, chemistry and medicine, centuries before most of the modern people of the world ever woke to civilized life. But, thereafter, Indian progress became stabilised almost at the same economic and cultural level for a long period and the Indian people did not progress appreciably.[1]

By introducing modern education in India, the British brought the Indian people in contact with the extensive and profound achievements of the modern west in the sphere of scientific and social scientific knowledge.[2] The introduction of modern education was an event of great historical significance for India. It was definitely a progressive act of British rule. Three main agencies were responsible for the spread of modern education in India. They were the foreign Christian missionaries, the British Government and the progressive Indians.[3] During the early days of the Company's rule, the promotion of education was not recognized as a duty of the Government.[4]

The most noteworthy Churchmen, who made contribution in this field after the Charter of 1813, was Alexander Duff (1806-1878). Duff's support of English education was an important factor in persuading Bentick to issue his famous Resolution of March 7, 1835, which announced the new policy of the Government in favour of English education. His example influenced also the policy of the various missions in India. All over the country colleges supported by the missionary societies sprang up to teach western literature and western sciences. In Bombay, the Wilson College (1832), in Madras, the Christian College (1837), in Nagpur, the Hislop College (1844), in Agra, the St. John's College (1853), in Masulipatam, the Noble College (1841), were all established on the lines of Duff's "General Assembly's Institution" (1830) which was later amalgamated with the Scottish Churches College, Calcutta.[5]

Primary education had lagged behind partly because the state failed to act up to its own decisions, partly because the vast masses of India were so poor as to be incapable of sharing the expenses of its expansion. On the other hand, the progress of secondary education during the first phase of educational expansion in the nineteenth century was much more satisfactory. Collegiate education during the later half of the nineteenth century made no less rapid progress. Three examining and affiliating Universities were founded in 1857.[6]

A review of the progress of western education in the nineteenth century reveals how far-reaching its effects were in translating the Indian mind. With the spread of Western education, the position entirely changed. An acute consciousness and a perfect awareness on the basis of exploitation grew up among the classes. The sparks and slogans borrowed from the west began to expose the dark corners of the British rule, strengthening at the same time, the cry and clamour for redress.[7] As early as 1860, Rev. J. Long, giving evidence before the Indigo Commission testified :

English education, happily spreading in the country among

> the natives, is giving them a sense of freedom, leaving their minds with a regard to a sense of justice and imparting to them an English tone of revulsion against oppression. It is also welding the natives of the different Presidencies into one patriotic mass, with community of feeling in Indian subjects.[8]

The first and foremost factor that gave birth to nationalism was the Western learning and English language. Western education taught to the Indians what it was to be a nation. The chains of caste and orthodoxy were lessened.[9] Thousands of young Indians studied the political ideas of Burke, Herbert Spencer, Macaulay, John Stuart Mill, Locke, Rauseau, Mazzini, Cavour, Voltaire, and were imbued with the ideas of liberty, equality, fraternity, self determination and national freedom. They read about the French Revolution and their political consciousness was aroused.[10] About Western education, Dadabhai Naoroji, the Grand old man of India, wrote, "New light had been poured on us, teaching us the new lesson that Kings are made for the people and not the people for the Kings."[11] K.M. Panikkar has pointed out that the introduction of Western learning brought about a profound intellectual transformation in India.[12] Raja Ram Mohan Roy, Dadabhai Naoroji, W.C. Banerjee, Surendernath Banerjee, Pherozshah Mehta, Gopal Krishan Gokhale and D.E. Wacha were all educated in Western learning and they became the first pioneers of Indian Nationalism.[13]

While Western education and socio-cultural renaissance were inculcating the educated people with new thoughts and ideas, there was yet another and a more powerful agency at work, silently moulding and shaping public opinion on a much larger scale throughout the country. That was the Indian Press.[14] In modern times, the Press had become a powerful social institution. This is proved by the fact that the press had been glorified as the Fourth Estate. The Press was a formidable weapon in the hands of the European people in the seventeenth, eighteenth and nineteenth centuries, in integrating themselves as nations, in organising struggles against feudal disunity maintained by the feudal nobility, and in establishing the modern national state, society and culture.[15]

The Press became an indispensable weapon for the rising social forces led by the intelligentsia including political writers such as Mirabeau, Danton, Robespierre, Marat and others, to stir up the consciousness of the people, to enlighten it with new ideas and lead them through a great historic struggle for the overthrow of the feudal state and society and replace them by the modern national state and society.[16]

The introduction of the printing press in India was an event of revolutionary significance in the life of the Indian people.[17] In 1767, the first attempt was made to start a newspaper, but the author, William Bolts, was deported. In 1780, however, James Hicky founded the *Bengal Gazette* and this was followed by *Madras Courier* in 1785 and *Bombay Gazette* in 1789. These were primarily official organs.[18]

Raja Ram Mohan Roy was the founder of nationalist press in India. Though a few papers had been started by others before him his *Sambad-Kaumudi* in Bengali published in 1821 and *Mirut-ul-Akhbar* in Persian published in 1822 were the first publications in India with a distinct nationalist and democratic progressive orientation. These papers were mainly the organs of the propaganda of social reform and a critical discussion of religious and philosophical problems. In Bombay, P.M. Motiwala started the *Jame-Jamshed* (Gujrati), which as a daily, is still being published, in 1831. Two more papers in Gujarati, *Rast-Gafter* and *Akhbar-e-Saudagar*, were founded in Bombay in 1851.[19]

Ishwar Chander Vidyasagar, the famous nationalist and social reformer, started the *Shome-Parkash* in Bengali in 1858. *The Times of India* was founded in Bombay in 1861. *The Pioneer* in Allahabad in 1865, *The Madras Mail* in 1868, *The Statesman* in Calcutta in 1875, and *The Civil and Military Gazette* in Lahore in 1876. All these papers were English dailies and persisted during the British period. The nationalist press also grew during this period. In Bengal the *Amrit Bazaar Patrika* was founded as an Anglo-Bengali weekly as the result of the combined efforts of the Ghose brothers, Hemendra Kumar, Shishir Kumar and Motilal in 1868. It was turned into English daily in 1891. The *Amrit Bazaar Patrika* propagated strong nationalist views and had been of one of the most popular of the nationalist newspapers.[20]

Under the advice of Sir Surendernath Banerjee, Sir Dyal Singh Majithia started *The Tribune* from Lahore, an English daily in 1877. It was an influential paper in Punjab with a liberal nationalist hue. The broadening and deepening of the nationalist movement after 1889 was reflected in the growth of the nationalist press, Tilak started *The Kesari*, a Marathi journal. Tilak was a journalist of consummate ability and, in his hands, *The Kesari* and *The Maratha* (an English weekly) became effective weapons to install militant nationalist sentiments and ideas among the people. Tilak was sentenced to imprisonment twice for his articles in *The Kesari*.[21]

The vernacular press was also rapidly expanding in India. *Jan Shakti, Anand Bazaar Patrika, Bangbasi* in Bengali, *Kesari, Lokmanya, Navakul* and *Kirloskar* in Marathi, *Bombay Samachar, Hindustan* and *Vandematram* in Gujrati, *Matribhumi* in Malayalam, *Swadeshamitram* in Tamil, these and others were some of the prominent dailies and weeklies in these languages.[22]

Though often critical of the Government policies during the first half of the 19th century, the Anglo-Indian press was bound by bonds of interests and sentiments to the British Indian Government.

This relationship, as also the resources commanded by it enable the Anglo-Indian press to develop rapidly in Punjab as well as in other parts of the country. In the beginning, *Delhi Gazette, Delhi Sketch Book* and the Sounder's monthly Magazine were in circulation throughout the country.[23] The most formidable Anglo-Indian paper in Punjab was the *Civil and Military Gazette*. However, soon after the passing of Punjab Land Alienation Act (1901), the press became quite vocal and started taking keen interest in the political events in the Punjab as well as in other parts of the country.

As regards the vernacular press though appearing on the scene of Punjab after the Anglo-Indian press, it rapidly developed in the second half of 19th century. In the year 1879, there were 29 vernacular papers in Punjab, only one *Mitra Vilas* of Lahore was in Hindi and the rest all were in Urdu.[24] It was the time when in Punjab, press acquired a place and standing as well as the maturity necessary for the growth inspite of the contrary expectation of the Punjab administration and Government.[25]

During 1881-82, there was a notable development in the press in Punjab. The strength of papers increased from 29 to 35. Soon after this period, there was a phenomenal growth of the press in Punjab as the Government began to supply official news to the newspapers.[26] Lahore was the most important centre in Punjab for the publication of newspapers, journals, weeklies, fortnightlies and the monthlies. *The Punjabi, Anjuman-i-Punjab* (1870), *Akhbar-i-Am* (1871), *Delhi Punch* of Munshi Nisar Ali, *Shuhrat* (1880), *Reformer* of Nathu Ram Anand (1880) were some of the important newspapers which were launched from Lahore.[27]

Since the Press was powerful weapon in the development of Indian nationalism and of the nationalist movement, it was subjected to restrictions by the British Government, which was reluctant to satisfy the aspirations and grant the demands of Indian nationalism. Indian nationalism, from its very inception, recognized the value of the press in rousing the people to national conciousness and put up a tenacious resistance to all attempts to curtail its freedom. The history of struggle for the freedom of the press had, therefore, been an integral part of the nationalist struggle. The freedom of the press was one of the basic democratic liberties which Indian nationalism, in all its stages of evolution, cherished and fought for.[28]

The challenge of the west to the basic ideas and institutions of the east was totally unprecedented. As the overwhelming domination of the authority of England in the political field appeared unshakable and efforts to dislodge it proved futile, attention naturally turned to the cultural and social aspects of Western domination. In the first decades of the nineteenth century, western impact had started the process of self-criticism and reform of religion. In the second half of the century the process acquired greater momentum. The challenge of the western Christianity had aroused both the Hindus and the Muslims to set their houses in order.[29]

In India, the first national awakening expressed itself in the form of a series of religio-social reform movements.[30] While Western education began to create in the country a new class of people interested in bringing about the emancipation of India, a few stalwarts of Indian thought and culture undertook the task of socio-cultural renaissance. These men were : Raja Ram Mohan Roy, Swami Dayanand Saraswati, Swami Vivekananda, Rama Krishna Paramhansa, Keshav Chander Sen, Mrs. Annie Besant and a few others.[31]

Raja Ram Mohan Roy was among the first few Indians, who formed his new ideas as a result of dissemination of western culture on the Indian soil. His approach in religious matters was largely intellectual.[32] He was a great rationalist like Martin Luther, Descarter and Bacon. While Roy was proud of India's past heritage and culture. He wanted the people to benefit from western science, technology and political thoughts as well as institutions.[33]

The Brahmo Samaj, established in 1828 by Raja Ram Mohan Roy. Here is rightly described as the father of Indian Nationalism. It was the first movement of this kind,[34] with the object of awakening the masses from their lethargy and backwardness. He was more a social reformer than a theologian or philosopher.[35] He attacked the polytheistic degeneration of ancient Hindu monotheism. His attack on polytheism and idolatry was motivated by national and socio-ethical considerations as much as by philosophical conviction. *The Brahmo Samaj* under the leadership of the Raja Ram Mohan Roy, launched an offensive against the caste system, branding it undemocratic, inhuman and anti-national institution. It crusaded against *satti* and child marriage. It stood for the freedom of the widow to remarry and equal rights of man and women.[36]

The Brahmo Samaj valued the modern western culture and organised educational institutions in the country for its spread among the people. *The Brahmo Samaj* was the pioneer of the nationalist movement, which began as a reform movement aiming at liberating the individual from the dead weight of an authoritarian religion, which strangulated their initiative and stultified both the individual and collective mind. *The Brahmo Samaj* inaugurated a new era for the Indian people by proclaiming the principles of individual freedom, national unity, solidarity and collaboration and democratization of all social institutions and social relations. It was the first organised expression of their national awakening.[37]

The temper which produced religious and social movements among the Hindus of Bengal and Maharashtra, as also among the Muslims of Northern India, the Parsis of Western India and others, was in fact characteristic of the whole of India. There had been a stirring of the spirit in all parts of the country and among all sections of the people. What happened in Bengal and Maharashtra, was repeated in Gujrat.[38]

In 1824, in a pretty state of Morni in Kathiawads, was born a child who grew into a reformer of an unusual type and of a different grain. Mul Shanker, the son of a Samvedi Brahman, who became famous under the name of Dayananda, was a child of a stern and rebellious mood. Dayananda was no ordinary person. His intellectual gifts were of a high order, in Sanskrit learning few surpassed him. He was an impressive speaker and a keen and ready-witted debater, who could overwhelm his opponents with a wealth of subtle arguments. His slogan was, 'Back to the Vedas', so for as spiritual and ethical life was concerned. *The Arya Samaj,* which he founded in Bombay in 1875 made rapid progress.[39]

The Arya Samaj had a programme of social reform also. Through opposed to the hereditary caste system, it stood, however, for the four caste division of society to be determined by merit and not by birth. *The Arya Samaj* stood for equal rights of man and woman in social and educational matters. This was a distinct democratic conception. *The Arya Samaj* organised a network of schools and colleges in the country, both for boys and girls, where education was imparted in the mother tongue. The Dayanand Anglo-Vedic College was founded in 1886. In all its activities, *the Arya Samaj* was generally inspired with the spirit of nationalism and democracy. *The Arya Samaj* represented a form of national awakening of the Indian people. It played a progressive role in the earlier stages, when the national awakening was just sprouting. *The Arya Samaj* had two characteristics, one progressive and the other reactionary.[40]

In Bengal, the reaction against westernisation had set in even before, by the formation of Ramakrishna Mission.[41] Ramakrishna Paramhans also played a significant role in Hindu renaissance. He was said to be in direct line of Chaittanya Mahaprabhu and was highly spiritual. Paramhansa's work was carried forward by his very able and devoted disciple, Swami Vivekanand. He was very much influenced by the writings of some western philosophers like Spinoza, Descartes, Hume, Darwin, Kant, Hegal and he proclaimed the oneness of all religions. By his teachings, Vivekananda created among the people a sense of confidence and self-reliance.[42]

Speaking at Madras, Vivekanand said, "The time has come for the Hinduism of the Rishis to become dynamic. Shall we stand by whilst alien hands attempt to destroy the fortress of the ancient faith. In order to rise again, India must be strong and united and must focus all its living forces."[43] The Ramakrishna Mission aimed at protecting India from materialist influences of western civilization. It idealized Hinduism including its practice of idol worship and polytheism. It aimed at the spiritual conquest of the world for revived Hinduism.[44]

The Theosophical Society under the leadership of Mrs. Annie Besant took up the task of Hindu revivalism in the South.[45] The Theosophical movement had many Western features such as the creation of a world brotherhood, study of laws of nature and the physical power of man.[46] This society was first formed in New York city by a Russian lady, Helena Petrovna Balavatsty and American national, Colonel Olcott, in 1875. Annie Besant, an Irish lady who had developed great love for India, came here in November 1893, and began to spread the teachings of the Theosophical Society. Educational institutions were set up in the South to bring about a new awakening among the people and Hinduism.[47] It denounced race and colour prejudices. As early as 1903, Mrs. Besant avowed her political faith in these words, "India must be governed on the basis of Indian feelings, Indian traditions, Indian thoughts and Indian ideas."[48] The Theosophical Society was a powerful factor in the awakening of pride and self-respect of Indians.[49]

The state structure built by Britain in India was, therefore, basically exercised to safeguard and develop the British interests. This brought Britain into conflict with the Indian people, and the various classes and groups composing it in varying degree, since the interests of the latter collided with the British interests. Nationalism was the outcome of this conflict of interests and it gave birth to various political movements in the country.[50]

In 1843, the 'British India Society' was set up in Calcutta to voice the grievances of the people. In 1851, the 'British India Association' was formed by men like Rajinder Pal Mitra and Ram Gopal Ghosh and for the first time in 1853, this association placed before the British Parliament proposal for participation of Indians in the Government. But the work of this association was interrupted by the uprising of 1857. In 1875, the 'East India Association' was formed in Calcutta and at about the same time, the 'Saravjanik Sabha' was set up in Poona. The People of Madras Presidency organised themselves in 1884 into a powerful and energetic association known as 'Madras Mahajan Sabha'. On 31 January 1885, a public meeting of the citizens of Bombay was convened by Pherozeshah Mehta, K.T. Talang and Badruddin Tyabji, who controlled the public life of the 'Western Presidency' and the 'Bombay Presidency Association' was formed.[51]

Such provincial political activities had prepared the ground for the creation of a political organization, which would embrace the whole of India and bring together in one body, the several provincial associations and politically conscious individuals scattered over the country.[52] At midday on Monday, 28 December 1885, 'very close to one hundred gentlemen' (actually 72) met in the hall of the Gokaldas Tejpal Sanskrit College and Boarding House in Bombay. They were attending the inaugural session of what was originally called the 'Indian National Union'. This name was given up soon after in favour of a new one by which the historic body is known to this day, 'The Indian National Congress'. This session thus marked the advent of a new era destined to see the fulfilment, in a little over sixty years of the Indian nation's urge for liberation, sovereignty and self-reliance.[53] A.O. Hume is generally regarded as the father of the Indian National Congress.[54]

In 1885, with the first sitting of the Indian National Congress, the whole of India felt the throbbings of a new life. It was the most remarkable event in India's history. For the first time, political unity was sponsored not by a central indigeneous or foreign government, but by a group of stout-hearted, forward looking sons of the motherland hailing from all parts of the country. The birth of the Indian National Congress was an unprecedented phenomenon in the political history of India.[55] The Bombay correspondent of the *London Times* reported (weekly edition 5th Feb. 1886) : "For the first time, perhaps India as nation met together. Its congeries of races, its diversity of castes, all seemed to find common ground in their political aspirations."[56]

Mrs. Annie Besant thus commented on the first Congress, "The first Congress dissolved leaving a happy and inspiring example of the fine work done and units demonstrated. India had found her voice. India was realizing herself as a Nation. Strange and menacing was the portent in the eyes of the some, splendid and full of hope in the eyes of others. The rosy fingers of dawn maidens had touched the Indian skies. When would her Sun of Freedom rise to irradiate the Motherland".[57]

The establishment of the Congress quickened the growth of political consciousness of the Indian people. The Congress itself was a visible symbol of their growing unity as a nation.[58] The Congress made a rapid progress and within a year of its existence became well known throughout the length and breadth of the country.[59] The first national assembly of Congressmen transacted a great deal of serious business during the course of three days (28-30 Dec.). Nine resolutions were passed. Of the two, Punjab delegate Muralidhar took an active interest in the debates, resolutions and as and when the occasion arose, he brought to the forefront the problems facing his province.[60]

The delegates to the Congress, as also other activists from in and outside Punjab spread the message of Congress to the Punjab, especially to the urban middle class elites. But before we try to understand their work and its impact in detail, it is pertinently necessary to see who the early leaders of the Congress in the land of Five Rivers were. In brief they were as follows :

Sr. No.	*Name*	*Religion*	*Urban/Rural*	*Education*	*Profession*
1.	Muralidhar	Hindu	Urban	B.A.B.L.	Political Leader
2.	Satyanand Agnihotri	Hindu	Urban	B.A.	Religious Activist
3.	Dyal Singh Majithia	Sikh	Urban	B.A.	Landlord
4.	Fazl-i-Husain	Muslim	Rural	B.A., L.L.B.	Political Leader
5.	Duni Chand (Lahore)	Hindu	Urban	B.A., L.L.B.	Political Leader
6.	Duni Chand (Ambala)	Hindu	Urban	B.A., L.L.B.	Political Leader
7.	Har Krishan Lal	Hindu	Urban	B.A.	Indust-rialist
8.	Lala Lajpat Rai	Hindu	Urban	B.A.	Political Leader
9.	Ruchi Ram Sahney	Hindu	Urban	B.A.	Social Admist
10.	Shradhanand	Hindu	Urban	B.A., L.L.B.	Political Leader

These were the top ten leaders, who spread the message of Congress. The first branch came up in the third week of January 1886 in Ambala. This was the first branch of Congress to have been opened not only in Punjab, but perhaps in the whole of the country.[61]

In the meanwhile, the Punjab Land Alienation Bill was introduced in the Imperial Legislative Council in 1899.[62] The object of the Bill was to restrict the sale and mortgage of lands in the Punjab, so that the money-lenders might not easily have them transferred in satisfaction of their decrees. The agricultural debtor had to pledge his harvest or land and the judicial system as in existence before the passing of the Bill afforded the money-lenders the means of rapidly realizing their dues. The proposed Bill prohibited the land sale except to a member of agriculturist caste.[63] Thus, the Bill affected the material interests of both the political leader and the money-lender, who happened to belong largely to the urban Hindu commercial community. The Bill represented a threat to their liberty to invest in land. Because of the opposition to the Bill, it was felt necessary to send a strong delegation to the Lucknow session of the Congress. At the Lucknow session of the Congress, Lala Muralidhar and Lala Kanhaya Lal made impassioned speeches and a resolution denouncing the Bill was passed unanimously.[64]

The Congress in its resolution regretted the introduction of the Bill into the Supreme Legislative Council, and recommended that this Bill preventing the alientation of agricultural land by sale or mortgage be suitably amended.[65] The opposition to the Bill in the Council was led by Harnam Singh, who represented the interest of land-owners and money-lenders.[66] But the Bill was passed inspite of the opposition of the Congress, the other political leaders and the press.

Meanwhile, the political situation within the Congress had also been changing because of the determination of Tilak and his group to wrest a constitution. In the 1904 session of Congress, attempts were made to rally the Punjabi dissenters by appointment of a Committee to draft a new constitution for the Congress. Punjab was represented on this Committee by Lala Lajpat Rai and Lala Harkrishan Lal.[67] At its session of 1905, Gopal Krishan Gokhle, the President of the Congress, condemned the partition of Bengal as well as the Curzon regime.[68] All sections of the Indian National Congress were united in opposing this position. During the anti-partition agitation, the ideas of swadeshi and boycott were voiced.[69] All the nationalist leaders like Tilak, Aurbindo Ghose, Bipin Chandra Pal and Lala Lajpat Rai organised a country-wide campaign through the press and platform to popularise the ideas.[70]

Consequently, the Punjab Politics took a new turn and the 25th session of the Congress was held at Lahore on 1909.[71] Interestingly, when differences arose between the moderates and the extremists inside the Congress, the British Government made an ardent endeavour to create a split in the Congress ranks.[72] The reforms of 1909 fixed the maximum strength of Legislative Council of other provinces at fifty while the strength of the Punjab remained thirty only. The real purpose of the reforms was to divide the nationalist's ranks and to check the growth of unity among the Indians by encouraging Muslim separatism.[73]

The 1909 Congress condemned the separate electorates for the Muslims as designed to aggravate communal differences. It considered the franchise to be illiberal and rooted in the distrust of the educated classes. It regretted that the non-official majorities in the provincial legislative councils had been rendered ineffective by the system of nomination. But the Congress gratefully accepted the Act of 1909 as a "fairly liberal measure".[74]

Lala Lajpat Rai, who was in England in 1909, considered the reform scheme as the most mischievous one that could be conceived in the present condition of India for it permanently divided the country into two hostile camps—Hindus and Muslims. He did not complain of the preference shown to the Muslims, but he condemned the principle which divided the country into two hostile groups.[75]

Of course the period from 1913 to 1919 had been of great political awakening in the annals of the Punjab history. The Gadar movement, the Kama Gata Maru episode, the Jallianwala Bagh massacre and other events changed the political scenario of Punjab. Meanwhile the First World War was waged in 1914 and it had a far-reaching impact on the minds of the elites in Punjab. So, the outbreak of the war was looked upon by the Punjabis as a very serious matter, "Pregnant with the most awful possibilities."[76] Even the Congress leadership offered total support to the war-effort of the British.[77]

In 1916, Muslim League held its session at Lucknow. The Indian National Congress also held its session at Lucknow in 1916. The Congress and League came to an agreement about the method of election of the councils and distribution of the seats. The most important feature of the Lucknow Pact was that the Congress agreed to the separate electorates for the Muslims as proposed in the Minto-Morely Reforms and the League accepted the Congress demand for *'swaraj'*.[78] In Punjab, meetings were held in Lahore in February, 1917 to affirm the support of the Punjabis to the Congress-League pact.[79] In Punjab, there occurred a series of revolutionary activities during the First World War. Montague's recommendations marked the end of an epoch and beginning of a new one.[80] In order to give a practical shape to these recommendations, Edwin Montague and Lord Chelmsford produced their scheme of Constitutional Reforms, which led to the enactment of the Government of India Act 1919. Under this Act, the provincial governments were given more powers by introducing the system of Diarchy. The Congress condemned this Reform Scheme in the Delhi session of 1918. Gandhiji gave a call for a forceful hartal on 6 April, 1919. The people responded with unprecedented enthusiasm. The arrest of Mahatma Gandhi at Palwal on 9 April and the deportation of Dr. Satya Pal and Dr. Kitchlew created mass awakening throughout India.[81]

The dawn of April 13, 1919 brought happiness for all on the eve of Baisakhi festival, but it was unknown that there would be a tragedy in store in disguise. A meeting was held in Jallianwala Bagh to protest peacefully against the recent firing.[82] It would be difficult to say about the exact number of audience present in the Bagh, but it was certain that the assembly was in thousands.[83]

General Dyer, who had set out at the head of 90 soldiers and a machine gun marched into the only open entrance of the Bagh and the crowd had no exit. He ordered to open fire without giving any warning to the masses.[84] In all 1650 rounds were fired. It would be difficult to mention the exact number of the casualties because many people gave different numbers, but it could not be denied that a considerable number of casualties took place. After the massacre strict orders were issued. Later on 15 April, 1919 martial law was declared in Amritsar and Lahore.[85] Gandhiji called the event as an unexampled act of barbarity, and as a protest he returned his 'Kaiser-i-Hind' title.[86]

Consequently, the occurrence of the events in the Punjab and the launching of Gandhiji's Non-Cooperation Movement in 1920 opened a new chapter in the political life of the country. The Non-Cooperation Movement also embraced the Sikh demands voiced in the Gurdwara Reform Movement. Sikhs felt the need to broaden the scope of their initial struggle for Gurdwara Reform and to join the larger movement of nationalism in the country.[87] The Sikh League at its annual session held in Lahore thus adopted the resolution of non-cooperation.[88]

Meantime the Punjab Legislative Assembly elections of 1923 were announced. Then, there emerged on the political scene a dynamic regional party, the Unionist Party (1923), which opposed the Congress. The Congress, a faction-ridden body, could not face the challenge of the new party and it lost its vigour and strength. In these elections the main contest was thus between the Unionists and the Congressmen. Many important leaders toured the province. The Unionists did their work wonderfully well. The Congress was naturally handicapped here. Even the election management of the

Congress could not measure up to the Unionists.[89] As a matter of fact from 1923 to 1927, Congress was hardly seen in any strong position anywhere.

This situation lasted up to 1927. This year a significant development made some difference. It was the appointment of the Statutory Commission on November 8, 1927, for the revision of the Constitution. The Commission comprised white men only and it had not even a single man representing Indian interest. The Congress decided to boycott it in its session held at Madras in December 1927.[90]

The Punjab Congress also decided to oppose the Commission with all the power at its command and surprisingly they did it better than could have been expected of them. As the days of arrival of the Commission drew nearer, the boycott movement gathered momentum. Posters like 'Punjab would not pocket the insult', 'Simon and Co. not wanted' and 'A Big Hoax' appeared at various places.[91] When the Simon Commission reached Lahore on 20 October, 1928, it was greeted with black flag demonstration and shouts of 'Simon, go back', by the huge crowd gathered at the Lahore railway station. The Police resorted to charge of lathis and battons, and caused severe injuries to a number of persons. Lala Lajpat Rai,[92] who was leading the procession, was allegedly beaten up by Mr. Scott himself, which led to his death on 17 November 1928. Lajpat Rai's death plunged the Indian people and leaders into deep grief and sorrow.

The Simon report was also not appreciated by the Sikhs. The nationalists had condemned the appointment of Simon Commission.[93] An all parties conference was convened in Delhi in 1928. The conference appointed a committee led by Moti Lal Nehru to evolve an agreed formula. An all parties' conference was held at Calcutta in December 1928 along with the Congress session to discuss the Nehru Report. A deputation of Sikh leaders led by Master Tara Singh met Gandhi. But there could not be any compromise.[94] As a result of this, the Central Sikh League withdrew the support to the Nehru Report and quit the Conference.[95] Before the Congress session began at Lahore, Dr. Ansari, Mahatma Gandhi and Pt. Moti Lal Nehru met Master Tara Singh, Baba Kharak Singh and other Sikh leaders and listened to their grievances.[96] They assured them that in future no proposal or decision would be acceptable to Congress, which did not satisfy the Sikh and Muslim minorities. A resolution to this effect was later on passed by the Congress in its Lahore session.

The Nehru Committee failed to produce any agreed document that could serve the future Constitution of India. The British Government called a Round Table Conference of Indian leaders at London on November 1930 to discuss basis of a new Constitution for Indians and the quantum of power to be transferred to Indians. However, Congress and Central Sikh League decided to boycott the first Round Table Conference.[97] On 5 March 1931, the Gandhi-Irwin Pact was signed and the Congress agreed to participate in the Second Round Table Conference.[98] Similarly the Central Sikh League also decided to participate. The Second Round Table Conference opened in London in September 1931. Like the First Round Table Conference a Minority Committee was again appointed.

The Conference arrived at no agreement and Gandhi returned empty-handed to the country. Gandhi addressed a conference at London in which he said that he was sorry that he had not been able to solve the communal problem.[99] As the Indians could not arrive at any settlement, Ramsay McDonald (Prime Minister of England) gave his famous award known as Communal Award on 16 August, 1932. The distribution of seats in the Punjab as awarded was :[100]

	Seats	*Percentages*
1. Muslims	86	49.14%
2. Hindu	43	24.51%
3. Sikhs	32	18.29%

The Sikh leaders' reaction to the Award was sharp and bitter. It had given the Sikhs only 18.29% representation as against their demand of 30%. The Sikhs got nothing in the

United Provinces and Sindh, where they had then a sizeable population.[101] Sampurn Singh and Ujjal Singh marked their protest by resigning from the constative committee of the Round Table Conference. In 1932, a new organization known as 'Khalsa Darbar' representing all sections of the Sikhs was also formed to lead an agitation against the Award.[102]

The Akalis asked the Congress to support them against the Communal Award. But the Congress instead of helping them adopted a neutral attitude. In this way, it was only after the condemnation and abandonment of the initial policy of neutrality towards the Communal Award by Jawaharlal Nehru on 2 June, 1936 that the Congress got some strength in the Punjab.[103] By doing so he removed the main cause of the Sikh and Muslim grouse. He further said, "I am for independence and so is the Congress and neither I, nor the Congress accept the Award."[104]

The Communal Award was followed by the Third Round Table Conference, which was held in London from 17 November to 24 December, 1932. Only 46 Indian delegates without the leaders of Congress participated in this Conference. After the conclusion of the Conference, the British prepared its Draft Scheme of Constitutional Reforms, which was published in the form of a White Paper in March, 1933. Of course the Communal Award and White Paper continued to be the central theme of the Punjab politics of another year.[105]

Meanwhile, the Joint Select Committee of both the Houses of British Parliament under the Chairmanship of Linlithgow, was considering the future of constitutional reforms in India with special reference to the proposal contained in the White Paper. The recommendations of the Joint Select Committee led to the decision of the British Government to pass the Indian Act of 1935, introducing some further constitutional reforms. The new Act proposed a federal government at the Centre and provincial governments in the eleven provinces with large measures of autonomy.[106]

The stage having been set for the elections in Punjab, about 775 candidates belonging to different parties participated in the election fray.[107] Polling took place from 18 January to 13 February, 1937.[108] It was expected before the elections that the Congress would sweep the polls in the Hindu dominated areas. But in the election results, the Unionist party emerged as the single largest party with a clear majority in the provincial assembly.[109] With the absolute majority of the Unionist Party in the Punjab Legislative Assembly Sikander Hyat Khan formed the ministry in Punjab with the help of National Progressive Party and Khalsa National Party. Sunder Singh Majithia, the leader of the Khalsa National Party, joined the new ministry. Later on, Sikander Hyat Khan joined the Muslim League due to Muslim pressure.

The Akalis who had been involved in the Shaheed Ganj Gurdwara agitation felt perturbed over Punjab Premier joining League due to Muslim dominations in the Punjab. To counteract the Muslim League's influences, the Shiromani Akali Dal's executive passed a resolution in their meeting held on 27 October, 1937, exhorting the Sikh masses to join the Indian National Congress.[110] The Pact brought the Akalis and the Congress leaders formally closer to one another. In November 1938, when the All India Akali Conference was held at Rawalpindi, the Akali and Congress flags were hoisted together.

After the outbreak of the World War II in 1939, the British War Cabinet sent Stafford Cripps to win over Indian support for the War.[111] The Congress Working Committee in its resolution on 2nd April, 1942 turned down the Cripps proposals, because of the novel principles of non-accession for a province. The Committee gave to the country the slogan of 'Quit India'.[112] Maulana Azad, in his Presidential address, said, "The slogan 'Quit India' means nothing more and nothing less than the complete transfer of power to Indian hands."[113] The climax came with Gandhiji's speech late in the evening on the 8th August. In clear and firm tone, he asked the British to Quit India and at the same time told the Indians to either 'Do or Die'. It was this speech of Gandhiji, which gave birth to two famous slogans 'Quit India' and 'Do or Die'. The 'Do or

Die' slogan electrified the nation and on 9th August, the movement came into existence.[114]

In early morning of 9th August Gandhi, Nehru, Azad, Rajindra Prasad, Patel, Kripalini, Asif Ali, Pant and some other top ranking Congress leaders were arrested simultaneously throughout the country and a wholesome round up of important Congressmen took place. The All-India Congress Committee and Provincial Congress Committees were declared unlawful.[115]

Sikh leaders Master Tara Singh and Giani Kartar Singh were against the participation in the movement and had to leave the Congress. But Gurmukh Singh Musafir, Udham Singh Nagoke, Ishar Singh Majhail, Darshan Singh Pheruman and Sohan Singh Jalusman supported this movement. The third session of all India Akali Conference was held at Village Udowall in Lyallpur district on 26 and 27 September, 1942.[116] In one of its resolutions, the Akali Conference demanded the independence of India and an end to the political deadlock by the British Government.[117] In order to counteract the Muslim League's demand for a sovereign Muslim State, the Shiromani Akali Dal put forward the demand of the Sikh State.[118]

The main aim and the prominent feature of this demand was to insist upon the partition of the Punjab. The Akalis primarily stood for united India and wanted Azad Punjab only if Pakistan was to be formed. Gopal Singh has asserted, "No Sikh leader ever demand a sovereign Sikh State. This was only to counterblast to Jinnah's demand for Pakistan on the basis of religion."[119]

Meanwhile, the World War II came to an end and the British Government sought to reach at some solution to the Indian problem. Prime Minister Atlee's Labour Government took office on 26th July, 1945 and began to expedite matter towards full self-government. Elections to the provincial assemblies were announced on 21 August, 1945. In these elections, Muslim League won largest number of seats *i.e.* 75 out of 175, the Congress came out second with 51 seats including 10 Sikh seats, the Akalis won 22 seats and the

Unionists won only 20 seats.[120] The League, however, needed the support of another party in 175 member assembly to form the government, but a compromise could not be affected with the Congress and Akalis. So an Akali-Congress-Unionist coalition under Khizer Hyat Khan took over the government in March 1946.

Events moved fast during the last year of colonial rule. Meanwhile on 20 February, 1947, Prime Minister Atlee had announced his government's decision to hand over power to Indians latest by June 1934.[121] The new Viceroy Lord Mountbatten took over on 24 March to effect the transfer of power. Within a month of his arrival, it became clear to all concerned that the division of the country between India and Pakistan could not be averted. Congress party passed a resolution in a meeting on 6-8 March, 1947, and accepted the partition of Punjab.[122]

REFERENCES

1. A.R. Desai : *Social Background of Indian Nationalism,* Popular Prakashan, Bombay (1948), p. 135.
2. *Ibid.,* p. 136.
3. *Ibid.,* p. 139.
4. *Imperial Gazetteers of India,* Vol. VI, pp. 472-74.
5. Tara Chand : *History of the Freedom Movement in India,* Vol. III, Publication Division, Ministry of Information and Broadcasting, Government of India, New Delhi (1972), p. 181.
6. *Ibid.,* pp. 436-38.
7. M.M. Ahluwalia : *Freedom Struggle in India (1858-1909),* Ranjit Printers and Publishers, Delhi (1965), p. 178.
8. Evidence of *Rev. J. Long,* 12.6.1860, *Indigo Commission Report,* 1860.
9. H.H. Dodwell : *A Sketch of the History of India from 1858 to 1918,* London (1925), pp. 1213.
10. D.C. Gupta : *National Movement and Constitutional Development,* Vikas Publishing House, Delhi (1970), p. 19.
11. See Dadabhai Naoroji's Speech read on 2 May, 1867 before the East India Association in Chuni Lal Lallubhai Parekh (ed.) :

Essays, Speeches, Addresses and Writings of Dadabhai Noaroji, Bombay (1887), pp. 26-45.

12. K.M. Pannikar : *A Survey of Indian History*, Asia Publishing House, Bombay (1954), p. 205.
13. D.C. Gupta : *Op. cit.*, p. 20.
14. *Ibid.*, p. 28.
15. A.R. Desai : *Op. cit.*, p. 221.
16. *Ibid.*, p. 222.
17. *Ibid.*, p. 223.
18. D.C. Gupta : *Op. cit.*, p. 28.
19. A.R. Desai : *Op. cit.*, pp. 224-25.
20. *Ibid.*
21. *Ibid.*, pp. 225-26.
22. *Ibid.*
23. Imperial Record Department, Newspapers List of Mutiny Papers, for further details see Tara Chand : *Op. cit.*, p. 451.
24. R.P. Bhatnagar : *The Rise and Growth of Hindi Journalism*, Allahabad (1947), p. III.
25. *'The Vernacular Press'*, Contemporary Review, Vol. XXXVIII (1880), p. 473.
26. *Aftab-i-Punjab* (Lahore) July 24, 1882, RNN, NWP and Punjab, (1882).
27. K. Sajan Lala : *A Short History of Urdu Newspapers*, Hyderabad (1964), p. 2.
28. A.R. Desai : *Op. cit.*, p. 230.
29. Tara Chand : *Op. cit.*, p. 391.
30. A.R. Desai : *Op. cit.*, p. 286.
31. D.C. Gupta : *Op. cit.*, p. 21.
32. Tara Chand : *Op. cit.*, p. 393.
33. D.C. Gupta : *Op. cit.*, p. 22.
34. A.R. Desai : *Op. cit.*, p. 287.
35. D.C. Gupta : *Op. cit.*, p. 22.
36. A.R. Desai : *Op. cit.*, p. 290.
37. *Ibid.*

38. *Ibid.*, p. 421.
39. Tara Chand : *Op. cit.*, p. 423.
40. A.R. Desai : *Op. cit.*, p. 292.
41. M.M. Ahluwalia : *Op. cit.*, p. 223.
42. D.C. Gupta : *Op. cit.*, p. 24.
43. G.C. Narang : *Real Hinduism*, New Delhi (1966), p. 188.
44. A.R. Desai : *Op. cit.*, p. 293.
45. D.C. Gupta : *Op. cit.*, p. 23.
46. M.M. Ahluwalia : *Op. cit.*, p. 220.
47. D.C. Gupta : *Op. cit.*, p. 23.
48. Geoffery West : *Life of Annie Besant*, Gerald Howe Ltd., London (1929), p. 206.
49. Tara Chand : *Op. cit.*, p. 426.
50. D.C. Gupta : *Op. cit.*, p. 33.
51. *Ibid.*
52. Tara Chand : *Op. cit.*, p. 545.
53. *A Centenary History of the Indian National Congress (1885-1985)*, Vol. I, Vikas Publishing House, All India Congress Committee, Delhi (1985), p. I.
54. Prakash Chandra : *History of the Indian National Movement*, Vikash Publishing House, Delhi (1997), p. 31.
55. Tara Chand : *Op. cit.*, p. 549.
56. *Proceedings of Indian National Congress*, Repoıt of the first session of the Congress, (1885), p. 153.
57. K. Ishwara Dutt : *Congress Encyclopedia*, Vol. I, p. 15.
58. A Centenary History of the Indian National Congress (1885-1985) : *Op. cit.*, p. 108.
59. Dr. P.N. Chopra, Ram Gopal and Dr. M.L. Bhargava : *A Century of the Indian National Congress (1885-1985)*, Agam Prakashan, Delhi (1986), p. 30.
60. A.C. Banerjee : *Indian Constitutional Documents*, Vol. II, Calcutta (1961), pp. 31-67.
61. K.C. Yadav : *The Builders of Our Nation : Muralidhar*, Vol. I, Kurukshetra (1987), p. 56.

62. N.G. Barrier : *The Indian Economic and Social History Review*, January 1965, Vol. II, No. 1, pp. 146-61.
63. Malcolm Darling : *The Punjab Peasant in Prosperity and Debt*, Delhi (1977), p. 156.
64. *Report of the Fifteenth Indian National Congress Session*, Lucknow, (1899), pp. 44-47.
65. *The Tribune*, December 19, 1899, p. 3.
66. B.B. Mishra : *The Indian Middle Classes*, Oxford University Press, New Delhi (1978), p. 355.
67. Purushotam Nagar : *Lala Lajpat Rai*, Manohar Book Service, Delhi, (1977), p. 17.
68. Shankar Ghose : *Congress Presidential Speeches*, AICC, New Delhi, (1975), pp. 24-29.
69. Dhanpatti Pandey : *The Arya Samaj and Indian Nationalism*, New Delhi, 1972), p. 107.
70. Purushotam Nagar : *Op. cit.*, p. 30.
71. Azim Husain : *Fazl-i-Hussain : A Political Biography*, Bombay (1946), p. 70.
72. Bipan Chandra, Amales Tripathi and Barun De : *Freedom Struggle*, New Delhi (1972), p. 75.
73. *Ibid.*, p. 100.
74. *Report of Twenty-Fifth Indian National Congress*, 1909, Lahore, pp. 1-2.
75. J.S. Dhanki : *Lala Lajpat Rai and Indian Nationalism*, ABS Publications, Jullundhar (1990), pp. 79-80.
76. Raja Ram : *Impact of First World War on Punjab*, (unpublished Thesis) P.U., Chandigarh (1972), pp. 5-8.
77. Andrews and Mukharjee : *Rise and Growth of Congress*, Meerut (1967), pp. 146-47.
78. The Congress-League Scheme is discussed in *Home Department Political* (A) File no. 25-1-259, pp. 30-32.
79. Azim Hussain : *Op. cit.*, p. 89.
80. *Report on the Constitutional Reforms*, Calcutta (1918), p. I.
81. *The Tribune*, Lahore, 9-12, April 1919.
82. *Report of the Disorder Inquiry Committee* 1919-20, Vol. II, p. 398.

83. Of prior to the arrival of General Dyer, the audience was estimated at 20,000. *Report of the Congress Inquiry Sub-Committee*, p. 54.
84. *Report of Disorder Inquiry Committee*, p. 44.
85. *Home Department Political* (B) May 1919, Proceedings No. 80, 82, 83, 85, 90, 93 and 95.
86. Velentine Chirol : *India : Old and New*, Eastern Bean Ltd., London (1926), p. 207.
87. Mohinder Singh : *"Aklis and the Non-Cooperation,"* Proceedings Punjab History Conference, Patiala (1978), pp. 174-75.
88. *Home Department* (Political Deposit), Government of India Proceedings, December 1920, No. 59.
89. *The Indian Year Book*, 1924, Calcutta (1924) *(NAI) Home Department*, Public File No. 952/1924, pp. 95-97.
90. *The People*, November 22, 1928.
91. *The Tribune*, December 6, 1928.
92. Lala Lajpat Rai said in his speech on 31 October, *"Every blow hurled at us was a nail in the coffin of British Empire."*
93. M.S. Sahni : *Sikh Politics (1927-47)* (unpublished Ph.D. Thesis) Punjabi University, Patiala, p. 20.
94. *The Tribune*, Lahore, 26 December, 1928.
95. *Ibid.*, 29 December, 1928.
96. *The Collected Works of Mahatma Gandhi*, Navjivan Publishers, Ahmedabad (1968), Vol. 42, pp. 326-27.
97. Harjinder Singh Dilgeer : *Shiromani Akali Dal—Ik Itihas*, Punjab Book Co., Jullundhar (1978), p. 120.
98. M.S. Sahni : *Op. cit.*, p. 134.
99. Durlab Singh : *The Valliant Fighter*, Meo Publications, Lahore (1942), p. 90.
100. *Home Political*, File No. 41/1-32, G.O.I., quoted in M.S. Sahni : *Op. cit.*, p. 144.
101. Kushwant Singh : *A History of the Sikhs, 1839-1974*, Vol. II, Oxford University Press (Indian Edition), Delhi (1977), p. 60.
102. *The Akali Te Pardesi*, 31 January, 1932.
103. *The Tribune*, Lahore, 3 June, 1936, see also S. Gopal (ed.) :

Selected Works of Jawaharlal Nehru, Vol. 8, New Delhi (1972-79), p. 131.

104. *I.A.R.* (1936), Vol. I, p. 360.

105. Lajpat Rai Nair (ed.) : *Sikander Hyat Khan : The Soldier Statesman of the Punjab,* Lahore (1943), pp. 13-14.

106. Bipan Chandra, Amales Tripathi and Barun De : *Op. cit.*, pp. 189-90.

107. *The Tribune,* Lahore, 4 December, 1936 and 7 February 1937.

108. Satya M. Rai : *Legislative Politics and the Freedom Struggle in the Punjab, 1897-1947,* New Delhi (1984), pp. 222.

109. Party wise position in the Punjab Legislative Assembly

Party	*Seats won*
1. Unionists	98
2. Congress	18
3. Khalsa National Party	13
4. Hindu Mahasabha	12
5. Akali Party	11
6. Ahrars	02
7. Itihad-I-Millat	02
8. Muslim League	02
9. Congress Nationalist	01
10. Independents	25

Source : NMML, File L-23/1937.

110. K.C. Gulati : *The Akali : Past and Present,* Ashajanak Publications, New Delhi (1974), p. 77.

111. Draft Declaration for discussions with Indian Leaders (as published) March 30, 1942, T.P. V.I.D. 456, P. 565 quoted in Indu Banga : *Crisis of Sikh Politics, 1940-47,* p. 239.

112. *I.A.R.,* Vol. II, 1942, pp. 209-11.

113. *Ibid.*, p. 237.

114. R.R. Diwakar : *The Quit India Movement* in *The Tribune,* Chandigarh, 9 August, 1987.

115. Y.B. Mathur : *Quit India Movement,* Delhi (1979), p. 71, also see *Home Political* File No. 3/16/1942 Poll (I) Part 1.

116. *I.A.R.*, Vol. II, (1942), p. 297.

117. *Ibid.*, p. 301.

118. Sadhu Singh Hamdard : *Azad Punjab*, Ajit Book Agency, Amritsar (1943) (Urdu), p. 48.

119. Gopal Singh : "*The Sikh Situations, 1847-1947*," Punjab Past and Present, Vol. XVI, No. 2, October 1942, p. 480.

120. The Party position in the Punjab Assembly was as follows :

1946 Election Results

Party	*Muslims*	*Hindu*	*Sikh*	*Total*
Muslim League	75	—	—	75
Congress	01	40	10	51
Akali Dal	—	—	22	22
Unionist Party	15	04	—	20*
Independents	—	—	—	07

*Including One Christian.

Source : Home Political (1) 1946, File No. 79/1946, Vol. III, pp. 223-26 *(NAI)*.

121. V.P. Menon : *Transfer of Power in India*, Princeton University Press, Princeton (1957), Appendix IX, pp. 507-08.

122. *Ibid.*, p. 34.

2

Congress : A Mobiliser

The history of the Indian National Congress is closely associated with the history of Indian freedom movement. Though, according to some historians the movement began with the uprising in 1857, cynically called the "Sepoy Mutiny' by the alien chroniclers, its organizational manifestation was for the first time perceptible in the birth of the 'Indian National Congress' in 1885. Mr. Allan Octavian Hume is considered to be the father of the Indian National Congress.[1]

Beginning with faith in the benevolence of British rule, within a generation it had moved forward to demand self-rule. Less than thirty years had passed since the revolt, when a new generation of Indians, inspired with new ideas and thrilled by the vision of a new India came together and started a movement, which in sixty years attained its goal.[2] Only 72 delegates attended the first session of the Congress. But in course of time, they began to grow, both in volume and content and in less than two decades, the Congress began to draw the attention of the masses. Its doors were opened to all and it knew no difference between 'British India' and 'Indian India', between one province and another, between the classes and the masses, between the rich and the poor, between towns and villages, between agricultural and industrial interests and between castes and communities.[3]

It proclaimed the advent of a new era, the era of political unity, not imposed from above, but the expression of the deliberate will of the people.[4] The Congress made a rapid progress and within a year of its existence became well known throughout the length and breadth of the country.[5] The Indian National Congress received tributaries from all over the country and became the established political mainstream of the land. There were few persons of standing in any part of the country, who did not owe allegiance to it.[6]

The Congress party started its activities in Punjab immediately after its inception. The organisational structure of the party assumed shape after the first branch of the Congress was opened at Ambala. Prominent Punjabis participated in the annual session of the party as well as organized provincial meetings to strengthen the party set up at the local level. Gradually with the passing of the time, the party cadre emerged, which made the activities and programmes into mass movement. The Congress party in Punjab and its leaders took notice of the national as well as of the provincial issues, and they raised their voice on these issues at different platforms. From time to time, they successfully mobilised the people on number of political and social issues. Although other smaller political outfits and parties also operated on the political scene in Punjab, but it was only the Congress party, which had such a mass base and organisational structure in the province.

Punjab's participation in the Indian National Congress began as early as 1885. The delegates from Punjab, nevertheless, played an active part in the discussions of the resolutions placed before the meetings.[7] In the very first session, Lala Muralidhar, one of the five delegates from Punjab, moved a resolution that the various resolutions passed at the meetings of the Indian National Congress may be communicated to the political associations in each province and they may be requested to adopt such measures as they considered calculated to advance the settlement of various questions dealt within these resolutions.[8] It appears that the active participation of the Punjabis in the deliberations of the Indian National Congress was almost always accompanied by their concern for the provincial and sometimes, even their caste or communal interests.

The Alienation of Land Act, thus, was one of the most important and, at the same time, the most controversial Acts passed by the Imperial Legislative Council for Punjab.[9] The Land Alienation Act was designed to protect the agriculturists from the clutches of the money lenders. The act succeeded in safeguarding the interest of cultivators, but it also sowed the seeds of racial separatism, in short, with the Land Alienation Act, ethnicity came to matter more than religion.[10] The Punjab Land Alienation issue was taken up by Punjab delegates in the Indian National Congress session at Allahabad in 1901. These Congress delegates were opposed to the passage of this act, as majority of them had urban background and sympathies with the non-agriculturist classes. The Congress in its resolution regretted the introduction of the bill in the Supreme Legislative Council. But this decision could not be endorsed at the next session at Lahore because of Muslim opposition.[11]

However, the awakening of the three major communities—Muslims, Hindus and Sikhs, marked a beginning of political mobilisation which led to radical changes in a hereto fore, politically passive and slumberous Punjab.[12] Prior to 1905, Punjab was so politically dormant that it could be described "as quiet and somnolent as any bureaucracy would wish".[13] But the unexpected and unwanted partition of Bengal in 1905 by Lord Curzon created some stir all over India. Moreover, the Land Colonization Act of 1907, in which water rates were to be enhanced, served as a catalyst for major protests. The combined effect of all these factors resulted in widespread resentment against the British rule. At this juncture nationalist leaders likes Ajit Singh, Lala Lajpat Rai and many others incited the people of all shades to fight against the foreign rule.[14]

The Agrarian Unrest of 1907 compelled the British to withdraw the Colonisation Bill. Lala Lajpat Rai and Ajit Singh suffered deportation for their leadership and support of the movement. This event heightened the political consciousness among the people of Punjab.[15]

The growing popularity of the Congress was clearly

revealed when the Congressmen assembled at Lahore for the sixteenth session of All India Organisation. However, similar enthusiasm was not witnessed among the urban people in Punjab when the Congress session took place here in 1909. The number of Punjabi delegates, who participated in this session was 76 whereas in 1893, their strength was 421. For the next few years, the popularity of the Congress was at low ebb in this region[16] and the activities of the provincial Congress did not amount to anything more than annual gatherings in which a few interested in movement participated.[17] In some recent writings, it has been argued that the national movement in Punjab remained weak in this phase because provincial leadership was more interested in issues, which concerned the interest of their sectarian communities.[18] It seems that prior to 1917, the Congress did not exist in the province as a significant political organisation.[19]

Meanwhile, the World War-I broke out in 1914. On behalf of the people of India, the Indian National Congress offered their willing cooperation to the British Government with the hope to get political and constitutional concessions.[20] The extremists, on the other hand, were vocal in demanding self-government as a condition for helping the British. Annie Besant started making efforts for bringing the Moderates and Extremists together on a single platform and she finally succeeded in the 1915 session of the Congress.[21] The Congress session of 1916 at Lucknow was the first united Congress since 1908.[22] At this time, Secretary of State Montague made a declaration in the British Parliament on August 20, 1917, giving out some promises of political and constitutional reform in India. His reform scheme known as the Montague-Chelmsford Reforms, provided for the introduction of diarchical system of government in the province.[23] The Delhi Congress of 1918 had condemned the Montague-Chelmsford Reform Scheme as totally unsatisfactory and insisted on the grant of provincial autonomy at once, but as concession to the moderate opinion, acquiesced in the reservation of law, justice and police to the existing administration for a period of six years.[24]

The Punjab delegates to the Delhi session moved a

resolution criticising the inferior position assigned to Punjab in the reform scheme, which maintained that Punjab was not yet fit for self government because it had not advanced equally with the other provinces and its condition was different from them.[25] Their other objection was to the assumption that Punjab did not have a sufficient number of men to administer the province if the scheme was passed. The Congressmen from Punjab raised their voice against these assumptions of the Government. They insisted that their province did not suffer from any disability to receive a different status in the proposed reform scheme.[26]

World War-I ended in 1918. The Congress was becoming convinced that the Government did not mean to come up to their expectations. Instead to arm itself for dealing with any untoward situation, the Government introduced the Rowlett Bills.[27] The bills invested the Government with extraordinary powers to suppress the right of defending of accused with the help of the counsel. These drastic measures, which the bills sanctioned, were summoned up in the slogan : no *daleel*, no *vakeel*, no *appeal*.[28]

Nevertheless, the Bills became laws in March 1919. At this stage, Gandhi made a resolve to employ the remedy of satyagraha for the redressal of the grievances of his countrymen. The date of the countrywide hartal and protest against the Rowlett Act was changed from 30th March to 6th April by Gandhiji. A complete hartal was thus observed at Amritsar on April 6, 1919. This meeting was attended by 50,000 people.[29] On 9th April, 1919 Michael O' Dwyer, ordered the arrest and deportation of Dr. Satyapal and Dr. Kitchlew.[30] It was a matter of coincidence that on the day of Doctor's deportation, Mahatma Gandhi was arrested at Palwal and the news of Gandhi's arrest was also flashed all over the country.

An unarmed, but a large crowd had gathered on 13th April at Amritsar in Jallianwala Bagh to protest against the arrest of their popular leaders. General Dyer surrounded the Bagh with his army unit, closed the exist points with his troops and then ordered his men to shoot into the crowd with rifles and machine guns. They fired till their ammunition was exhausted. The massacre of innocent people at Jallianwala Bagh evoked great resentment among the Punjabis.[31] It would be difficult to mention the exact number of the casualties because eye witness and other people gave varying numbers, but it could not be denied that a considerable number of causalities took place.[32]

The Punjab delegates to the special session of the Congress, held at Calcutta in 1920, played an important role in the passing of the resolution on non-cooperation. Lala Lajpat Rai presided over the session.[33] Gandhiji's resolution on non-cooperation was adopted by 1855 votes against 873 votes. On 1 August, 1920, the Congress blared the bugle of the non-cooperation against the British Government. Gandhiji was the supreme general who was entrusted with the full command of the Congress forces fighting the 'Satanic Government'.[34]

The Punjab Provincial Congress Committee accepted the principle of non-cooperation at its meeting on August 8th, 1920. The Punjab Provincial Congress endorsed the programme of non-cooperation in its session in October, 1920. A non-cooperation committee was formed in the province as a joint venture of the Congress, the Muslim League, the Khilafat Committee, the Sikh League and the Indian Association.[35] The Non-Cooperation Movement was pressed in the Punjab after the endorsement of the non-cooperation resolution at the Nagpur session held in December, 1920.

Following the decision to support the Non-Cooperation Movement, a large number of meetings were held, and resolutions were passed for the release of political prisoners (arrested during the martial law days), the condemnation of the majority report of the Hunter Committee and the recall of the Viceroy. For the first time, the working class too got involved in the freedom movement resulting in a number of strikes during the period. In a lightening strike, 17,000 employees of the North Western Railway at Lahore were involved. The strike ended after 48 days. At Multan, the strikers proposed that they should, hereafter, boycott the non-strikers and stop greeting them. People from all sections of the society were touched by the ferment in Punjab. The younger sections, from almost all communities, openly sided with the Congress and the Khilafat workers. The Central Sikh League adopted the non-cooperation resolution by a large majority. The unity among the three communities once again perturbed the Punjab administration.[36]

The movement had both negative and positive programmes. The former included the boycott of courts, legislatures, foreign cloth and educational institutions maintained or aided by the government.[37] Under the boycott of courts, notable leaders of the Punjab Congress, such as Lala Lajpat Rai, Duni Chand (Lahore), Agha Safdar, K. Santaram and many others renounced their practice.[38] By April, 1921, 41 lawyers had suspended their practice, although, the government contended that their number was much less.[39]

The boycott of the government aided schools and colleges was an important item of the programme of non-cooperation.[40] The first Punjab Student Conference was held at Gujranwala in January, 1921.[41] The conference passed a resolution welcoming the Congress resolution on non-cooperation. Lala Lajpat Rai and Chaudhary Ram Bhaj Datta made stirring speeches at the conference.[42] The Punjab Provincial Congress Committee appointed a Board of National Education to guide and control the programme of national education in the province.[43]

As to the boycott of the councils, provided in the Act of 1919, the people were persuaded not to enter the Councils. Almost all the Congressmen stood aloof, when the elections were held under the Reform Act of 1914.[44] As a result of their organised efforts, less than five percent of the total number of voters recorded their votes in Lahore. At Amritsar, the percentage was still lower. Similar reports had been received from various urban and rural centers in Punjab.[45]

The Punjab Government adopted several measures to suppress the Non-Cooperation Movement. All public meetings were banned under the Seditious Meeting Act.[46] The Congress and Khilafat organisations were declared unlawful.[47] Further, Lala Lajpat Rai, G.C. Bhargawa, Dr. Kitchlew, Sardar Sardul Singh Caveeshar and many other prominent Congress leaders were arrested in Punjab.[48]

On February 5th, 1922, when a Congress procession was fired upon at Chauri Chaura near Gorakhpur in U.P., the angry people rushed twenty-one constables and sub inspectors into a police station and set fire to the station with the men in it. They all perished in the flames. Taking this as a sign of the unpreparedness of the people for a non-violent struggle and considering that a violent struggle with the government would be unequal one, Gandhiji decided to suspend the movement. Consequently on February 12th movement was withdrawn.[49]

The Punjab Provincial Congress Committee, infact, was shocked by Gandhiji's decision and regarded it as 'a candid' admission of the surrender of the people to the bureaucracy in regard to the inalienable rights of man, mainly, freedom of speech and freedom of association.[50]

As the tenure of the first Legislature Council was about to finish, certain political parties started preparing for the ensuing elections to the second council. The elections to the second council were held in November, 1923.[51] After the results, the strength of each party in the second council was :[52]

S.No.	Party	Seats won
1.	Unionists	33
2.	Sawaraj Party	12
3.	S.G.P.C.	9
4.	Independents	17 (consisting Hindus 11, Muslims 5 and European 1)

On 24th April, 1926, the ban on the Congress and the Khilafat was lifted; such a ban was also lifted from Shiromani Gurdwara Prabandhak Committee and Akali Dal on 15th Sept., 1926. In the meantime, the elections to the third Legislative Councils were drawing near.[53] At this juncture, all the parties including Congress started girding up their loins for the elections.[54]

The Punjab Provincial Congress Committee issued an election manifesto in the beginning of November, 1926.[55] But Lala Lajpat Rai posed a great threat to the Congress, when he and Madan Mohan Malviya floated a new party, namely, the Nationalist Party in August, 1926 and in co-operation with the Hindu Sabha started working actively against the Congress candidates. The speeches of these leaders had greater appeal for the middle class Hindu voters in Punjab than that of the Congress candidates, whereas a number of Congress sympathizers and workers shifted their allegiance to the Hindu Sabha and Nationalist Party. The Hindu and Muslim Jats from Haryana switched over their loyalty to the Unionist Party under the leadership of Chhotu Ram. The atmosphere had been considerably marred by communal tension with the exit of Lajpat Rai and his followers from the Congress. Lajpat Rai's efforts in favour of the Hindu Sabha candidates made a great impact on the elections of 1926.[56]

The elections to the third Legislative Council were held in November, 1926.[57] In this council, the Unionist Party received a thumping majority with 31 members. Nationalist Party emerged victorious on 12 seats, Central Sikh League on 11 seats, the Khilafatists on 3 seats, the Congress on 2 seats and independents on 12 seats.[58]

Another issue of considerable significance, which came up before the third council, was the attitude to be adopted towards the Simon Commission.[59] In November, 1927, the Simon Commission was appointed to enquire into the Working of Reform of 1919 and to make recommendations. The Commission which consisted of 7 members was presided over by Sir John Simon. All its members were Englishmen. The Commission was boycotted by the nationalists on the ground that it had no Indian member. The All India Congress session was held at Madras in December 1927. It passed the resolution to boycott the Simon Commission. Similarly, the All India Muslim League and the Hindu Maha Sabha resolved to boycott the Commission.[60] The Working Committee of Shiromani Akali Dal met on 16th January, 1928 under Sardar Udham Singh

Nagoke and announced its decision to boycott the Commission.[61]

The Commission visited Lahore on 10th March, 1928 and 20th October, 1928.[62] Its visit was marked by hostile demonstrations by the political parties at the Lahore Railway Station. The Congressmen and the Akalis were prominent among the 3000 demonstrators on this occasion.[63] When the Simon Commission reached Lahore on 20th October, 1928, it was welcomed with black flags demonstration and shouts of 'Simon, go back', by the mammoth gathering at the railway station.[64] In order to disperse the crowd, the police resorted to charge of lathis. Lala Lajpat Rai, who was leading the procession against the Commission, received fatal injuries on the chest, which resulted in his death on 17th November, 1928.[65] The death of Lala Lajpat Rai aroused a wave of indignation against the British Government and the Punjab Police. Lala Lajpat Rai said in his last speech on 31st October, "Every blow hurled at us is a nail in the coffin of the British Empire."

The forty-fourth session of the Indian National Congress was held at Lahore on 29th December, 1929. The huge pandal, which could accommodate about fifteen thousand people, was packed to its utmost capacity.[66] Pandit Jawaharlal Nehru, who had been elected Congress President declared that he was a socialist and a republican and was no believer in kings and princes. He further said, "Independence for us means complete freedom from British domination and British imperialism. I do not think that any form of Dominion Status applicable to India will give us real power. The test of this power would be the entire withdrawal of the alien army of occupation and economic control. Let us, therefore, concentrate on these and the rest and follow".[67] On 31st December, 1929, Gandhiji introduced the historic Independence Resolution, which gave direction to the future Congress programmes. The developments moved the Congress leadership a great deal and they decided to go for 'Purna Swaraj' in their historic declaration on 2nd January, 1930.

Meanwhile, Gandhiji had launched his all India movement

of Civil Disobedience in 1930. On 6th April, 1930, Gandhiji, walking slowly, in grave solemnity proceeded to the seashore with eighty-four volunteers and others. After a ceremonial dip in the sea, he and his followers broke the 'Salt Laws' exactly at 6.30 p.m. by taking a lump of natural salt from a small pit. Thousands of people witnessed the ceremony of breaking the Salt Laws.[68] Immediately after breaking the Salt Laws, Gandhiji issued the statement that everyone who would take the risk of prosecution under the Salt Laws could manufacture salt whenever he wished and wherever it was convenient to him. And thus started the Salt Satyagraha, which was popularly known as the Civil Disobedience Movement.[69]

On 30 July to 7 August, 1930, the Congress Working Committee met at Bombay to decide future programme of the Congress. It directed all Congress organisations to take steps to carry out as far as possible the following programme in the coming month :[70]

Boycott of foreign cloth. Boycott of liquor and other intoxicants. Boycott of central and provincial legislature. Boycott of British goods. Withdrawal of deposits in Post Office, Saving Bank Account and Post Cash Certificates. Boycott of government loans. Boycott of government officials. Disobedience of the various repressive ordinances. Preparation for and inauguration and continuance of a campaign for non-payment of land revenue or such other government taxes as the provincial organisation might consider necessary and feasible. Setting up in cooperation with the mercantile community arbitration boards for the purpose of dealing with the business disputes and the question of mutual payments. Calling upon students of colleges to take full share in the national struggle, even by suspending studies. Withdrawal of support of British Insurance, Banking and Shipping Concerns and Vigorous propaganda for the use of Swadeshi articles and support to Swadeshi concerns even at a sacrifice.

Instructions issued at the central level by the Indian National Congress were duly reflected in the activities of its provincial branch in Punjab. The Punjab Congress started making earnest preparations and jumped into the fray in a big way. The sleeping tiger stood up and began to roar and it roared for four years 1930-1934.[71]

In June 1930, as suggested by the All India Congress Committee, the Punjab Satyagraha Committee decided to intensify the movement of boycott of foreign cloth. It asked all the Congress Committee to give notice to all the foreign cloth shops not to sell foreign cloth for three months. It was also decided to give permission not to pay taxes to those villages, which wished to stop payment of taxes.[72]

Vigorous propaganda was conducted in favour of the Swadeshi and the boycott of foreign cloth. Leaflets were distributed and processions were organised to collect foreign cloth from the houses and shops to be burnt at street corners and market places. Merchants were persuaded to sign pledge of not selling imported cloth and allowing the bales of foreign cloth to be sealed by the Congress committees. Volunteers, both male and female, picketed the foreign cloth shops, octroi posts and wine shops. When the volunteers failed to persuade the merchants by picketing, they resorted to performing *'siapa'* (wailing ceremony performed on the death).[73]

Side by side with the boycott and picketing, efforts were also made to popularise 'swadeshi' in Punjab. The Punjab 'Swadeshi Pracharak Sangh' was formed at Lahore in July, 1930.[74] A 'Swadeshi Bazaar' was organised on a big scale, at Lahore for a fortnight commencing from 30 November. Lala Faquir Chand, Advocate, was appointed, President of 'Swadeshi Bazaar Committee'. The idea behind the 'Swadeshi Bazaar' was to give wide publicity to the Indian products and to bring together the 'Swadeshi' manufacturers and the customers.[75]

In August 1930, as mentioned earlier, the Punjab Provincial Congress Committee included the picketing of liquor shops also in the programme and to stop sale of other intoxicants. The liquor shops were picketed at many places such as Lahore, Amritsar, Ferozepur, Rohtak, Bhiwani, Multan and Gujranwala. At Lahore, ladies took an active part in the picketing of liquor shops at railway station, Landa Bazaar, Gowal Mandi, Dhobi Mandi, Lahori Gate, and English wine shops on the Mall.[76]

In the meanwhile, as the Civil Disobedience Movement in Punjab was going on, elections to the Punjab Legislative Councils fell due in September, 1930. As decided by the Punjab Congress Committee, efforts for picketing at elections were made at Sialkot, Ludhiana, Rohtak, Jullundhar and Ambala districts.[77] At Ludhiana, picketing was done by ladies, led by Kumari Vidyawati. A *'siapa'* or mourning ceremony was performed in front of one Mela Ram, an advocate of Ludhiana in consequence of his objection to the picketing of a polling station.[78]

In Punjab the Civil Disobedience Movement adopted the above-mentioned tactics, and boycott of the foreign cloth, particularly, had its effects. The Secretary of the Northern India Chamber of Commerce, informed the government of Punjab that a very grave situation had arisen as a result of the general repudiation of contracts by dealers in India in consequence of the boycott movement, enforced by picketing and the resultant total stoppage of trade.[79] The policy that the government followed to check the Civil Disobedience Movement was decided upon after a careful thought and consideration.

On 8 September, 1930, in exercise of the powers conferred by Section 16 of the Criminal Law Amendment Act, 1908, the Governor of Punjab declared the Punjab Provincial Congress Committee and the Lahore Congress Committee as unlawful associations.[80] Ultimately in September, 1930, it was decided that the Criminal Law Amendment Act, 1908, might be applied to all Congress Committees in the province with the object of breaking up the remaining organisation of the Civil Disobedience campaign with effect from 19 September 1930.[81] In Punjab, 7,189, persons were arrested on charges of illegal political activity.[82]

In the meantime, as the head of the administration in India, Lord Irwin, who had adopted a policy of repression in order to maintain law and order, also seemed to have realised that the sheer force would not cow down the patriotic impulse of the Indian people and that measurers of repression would serve no useful purpose.[83]

With the changed stance, the decks for the talks between the Viceroy and Gandhiji were clear. On 25th May, 1931, the ban on Congress Working Committee was withdrawn.[84] The Government of India cancelled the Punjab Governments notification of 28th August, 1930, declaring the Working Committees of the All India Congress Committee to be unlawful association, on 26th January, 1931.[85] It was under these circumstances, that Gandhiji sought an interview with the Viceroy, Lord Irwin, which he willingly granted. Negotiations for a settlement between Gandhiji and the Viceroy began on 17th February, 1931, and lasted up to 5 March, 1931, when the famous Gandhi-Irwin Pact was signed.[86]

The Gandhi-Irwin Pact was ratified by the Congress at Karachi. The Congress Working Committee, as it has been mentioned earlier, had already directed all Congress Committees to take immediate action in accordance with the Pact. Under such circumstances the atmosphere was rather peaceful.[87]

The Second Round Table Conference took place in September-December 1931. Gandhiji attended the conference as the sole representative of the Congress. The conference however, failed. In March 1933, it was decided by the Congress to hold its session in Calcutta on 31 March, 1933. The Government of India, however, decided not to allow it to hold the session, as the Congress still stood pledged to Civil Disobedience Movement. Nine hundred and thirty delegates including forty-six from Punjab were arrested in Calcutta between 28 March, 1938 and 1 April, 1938.[88]

In August, 1933, Individual Civil Disobedience was started, but it was not successful in Punjab. Dissensions among the Congress leaders, lack of funds, unwillingness among the Congress leaders and workers to go for imprisonment for the second and third time and many other factors were responsible for the low momentum during the second and final phase of the movement.[89]

The Punjab politics entered into a crucial phase with the announcement of the Communal Award. The Congress position of neutrality on the Award had a very damaging effect on its popularity among the Hindus, a section of the Sikhs and the Muslims nationalists of the province. In the Punjab Political Conference, held in 1935, the Award was condemned as "wholly unsatisfactory and anti-national". The delegates described it as "a challenge to Indian self-respect and source of growing inter-communal bitterness and dissensions."[90]

In the meantime, the Government of India Bill, with Communal Award as one of its main features, had received the Royal assent on August 2, 1935. The new Act was divided into two parts—one proposing a federation of Indian states and British Indian Provinces and the other conferring autonomy on the provinces.[91]

In India, the Act had more enemies than friends.[92] The Indian National Congress rejected it in its entirety. But the Congress decided to contest the elections in the provinces in order to combat it from inside and outside the legislature and render it inoperative.[93] The Congress formed a separate Congress Sikh Party for elections in Punjab with a view to widening the base of the national movement and for developing mass contact among the Sikhs.[94] Many Sikh Socialists, *Kirties* and others joined it and Sardar Sarmukh Singh Jhabbal was made the first President of the party.[95] The election tours of Jawaharlal Nehru in Punjab had strengthened the position of the Congress Sikh Party.[96] Meanwhile, the Congress had abandoned the initial policy of neutrality towards the Communal Award,[97] and removed the main cause of the Sikh grouse. The Congress manifesto declared :[98]

> The Communal decision, which forms part of the new constitution, had been rightly condemned as anti-national and anti-democratic. It will lapse with the constitution of which it is a part. The Congress in the meanwhile

endeavours to substitute for that decision or solution acceptable to all communities.

In the meantime, the Congress and the Akali Party reached a compromise with the ostensible object of combating the reactionary forces in the province.[99] The Akali Party decided to contest 14 seats and 10 seats were left for the Congressite Sikhs.[100] It was also decided that the Akali party in the legislature would form a part of the Congress in all political matters and would be amendable to the rules and discipline of the Congress.[101] The elections in the province were held in the beginning of 1937. The Unionist Party by getting 96 out of 175 seats of the Punjab Legislative Assembly, secured the majority.[102] The Congress obtained 18 seats and the Muslim League got only two. Among the Sikhs, the Khalsa National Party, secured 14 seats, the Akalis 10 and the Congressite Sikhs.[103]

With the absolute majority of the Unionist Party in Legislative Assembly, Sir Sikander Hayat Khan formed the ministry in Punjab. Sunder Singh Majithia also joined the new ministry.[104] The Akali Party strongly condemned Sunder Singh Majithia and his party for joining hands with the Government.[105] The Akalis described them as traitors and enemies of the 'panth.'[106] Besides, they alleged that the Khalsa National Party had accepted the programme of Unionist Party[107] and had conspired with the Government to crunch the growing power of the Akalis.[108]

In March, 1937, Nehru announced the formation of a Congress wing to organise mass contact with the Muslims and to convey the message of the anti-imperialist struggle to them. This persuaded the Nationalist Muslims, *Ahrars* and Ittehad-i-Millat to join hands with the Congress.[109] They played prominent roles. The Congress appealed to the Muslims of the province to strengthen it by enrolling themselves as Congress members in large numbers. By October, it had attracted thousands to its nationalist programme.[110]

The Congress further asserted that the Muslim mass contact drive did not mean any separate programme only for the

Muslims. But the doors of the Congress were open to all and particularly for those who wanted full freedom for their motherland and bread for her starving millions. They must join the Congress.[111] Akalis, Socialists and Communists not only whole heartedly supported the Congress programme, but also served in various Congress Committees in the province. At the success of this Muslims mass contact programme, the British Government saw danger to its power and the Muslim League saw danger to its solidarity and position in the country's politics.[112]

After the outbreak of the World War-II, the All India Congress Committee met at its historic annual session at Ramgarh in Bihar on 19 and 20 March, 1940 under the Presidentship of Maulana Abul Kalam Azad. The President devoted the best part of his presidential address to the communal question. He further blamed the British for pursuing a policy of divide and rule and exploiting their internal differences for consolidating their own power.[113] A historic resolution, approved by a vote of 2500 to 15, was passed at this session on 20 March. It declared :[114]

> The Congress considers the declaration by the British Government of India as a belligerent country, without any reference to the people of India and exploitation of Indian resources in war, as an insult intentionally to them, which no self-respecting and freedom-loving people can accept or tolerate. Under these circumstances, it is clear that the Congress cannot in any way, directly or indirectly, be party to the war, which means continuance and perpetuation of this exploitation. The Congress, therefore, strongly disapproves of Indian troops being made to fight for Great Britain and of the drain from India of men and material for the purpose of war. Neither the recruiting nor the money raised in India can be considered to be voluntary contribution from India.

The Congress Working Committee further made it clear that nothing short of complete independence could be accepted to the people of India.[115]

The Ramgarh session of the Congress was followed by the historic Lahore session of the Muslim League from 22 to 24 March. On 23 March, the League unanimously adopted the famous Lahore resolution popularly known as 'Pakistan Resolution'. The resolution was supported by the representatives from almost all the provinces.[116]

The 'Pakistan Resolution' was widely ridiculed and condemned in the Hindu and the Sikh press. The Hindu and the Sikh meetings were held in large numbers in protest. To the Sikhs, the Pakistan resolution came as a violent shock. They unanimously disapproved the idea of Muslim dominated Pakistan.[117] The reaction of the Congress towards the Pakistan Resolution was very sharp because it gave a severe blow to the conception of Indian unity for which the Congress had laboured hard up to this time. All the important leaders of the Congress like Gandhi, Nehru and Maulana Azad condemned it in strong words. The Working Committee of Punjab Provincial Congress met on 19 April and decried Mr. Jinnah and his resolution.[118]

The possibility of a Muslim State coming into being was more specifically recognised in the British War Cabinet's formula presented to India by Sir Stafford Cripps in 1942. The Cripps proposal offered to give Indian province the right to choose whether, they would join any union that might be formed at the end of the War or would stay out and form their own state, separately or in collaboration with other provinces similarly inclined. Pakistan had, thus, been clearly promised.[119]

The Congress rejected the proposals on the 2nd April. Gandhiji described the proposals as 'a post dated cheque on a crashing bank'.[120] The Sikhs turned down the scheme enunciated by Sir Stafford Cripps. In a representation to him, the Sikh All Parties Committee declared that the proposals were unacceptable to them for, "instead of maintaining and strengthening the integrity of India," specific provisions had been made for separation of provinces and the constitution of Pakistan and the cause of the Sikh community had been lamentably betrayed.[121]

Consequently, the Congress decided on the 14 July, 1942, at Wardha that a mass movement in support of its demand for independence should be launched under the leadership of Gandhiji. The All India Congress committee ratified this decision at a historic session, which was held on the 8 August at Bombay under the Presidentship of Maulana Abul Kalam Azad. The Committee gave to the country the slogan of 'Quit India'.[122] The 'Quit India' resolution signified the grim determination of the Congress to embark upon a life and death struggle for the liberation of India.[123]

Mahatma Gandhi had warned the people that Quit India Movement would be short and swift. There would be mass participation of the people. Each one would be his or her own guide. The Government would resort to brutal and ruthless repression. People would have to face the challenge non-violently in a spirit of 'Do or Die'.[124]

The British Government, however, was equally determined to be tough and ruthless. All the senior Congress leaders in Bombay were put under arrest and similar arrests were carried out in the provincial cities and district towns. The arrest of the Congress leaders triggered off a massive popular upsurge throughout India. In all the metropolitan cities, provincial capitals and district towns, the people rose in revolt against the British Government. In large parts of India, the centre of British administrative powers were overthrown and for the space of few weeks, British rule ceased to exit. The British Raj seemed to be in real danger of being overthrown.[125]

The sudden arrests of Congress leaders created a strong resentment amongst Congressmen in the Punjab. Large meetings were held in Lahore and Amritsar. Partial hartals in Lahore and Amritsar were observed on 10 and 11 August. At Amritsar, organised agitation, meetings and processions were banned under section 144. A minor clash with the police at Multan on the 11 August led to accidental death of three boys.[126] Though the movement reached its peak in the provinces like Bihar, United Provinces, North-West Frontier

Province, Central Province, Orissa and Sindh, yet its impact on the Punjab was relatively less.[127]

The 'Quit India' movement was, therefore, not as widespread in Punjab as in other provinces and according to official sources, by January 1943, even "the semblance of an organised campaign" had disappeared. This is, however, not true, for it was only the end of the first phase.[128]

Meanwhile, World War-II came to an end and the British Government sought to reach at some solution to the Indian problem. The circumstances took favourable turn for the independence of India. British Government sent to India a Cabinet Mission to effect the political settlement among the various parties of India. The Cabinet Mission reached Delhi on 24 March, 1946. The Mission held a series of discussions with the leaders of different political parties and the Governors of the provinces. However, the main parties dealt with, were the Congress, the Muslim League and the Sikhs.[129]

After discussions with Indian Leaders of different political shades, the Cabinet Mission presented a tentative scheme for discussion at a conference at Shimla in an effect to find a basis of agreement between the Congress and the League.[130] The Congress and Muslim League felt satisfaction at the report, but the Akalis were angry at it.[131] The Cabinet Mission left for England on the 29 June, because both the main parties, the Congress and the Muslim League—had agreed to accept the long term plan.[132] After the decision of the League not to join the Interim Government, Nehru assumed the charge of it on September 2. Sardar Baldev Singh took over the portfolio of Defence.[133] But the Congress leaders with their commitment to a centralised policy in India, feared that a confederal constitution would be merely a prelude to the Balkanisation of the subcontinent.[134]

To resolve the dilemma, Clement Atlee appointed Lord Mountbatton as Viceroy of India with plenipotentiary powers to resolve the constitutional impasse.[135] On 22 March, 1947, Lord Mountbatton took over as Viceroy from Lord Wavell. His brief was to arrange the transfer of power from British to

Indian hands as expeditiously as possile.[136] In a short span of time, he was able to establish relations of confidence with the leaders of the Congress and other parties. Mountbatton put before the Indian leadership a plan for the partition of India and the creation of two autonomous dominions from the province of British India. The Mountbatton plan, as it is popularly known, was a bitter pill for the Congress leaders to swallow since from the very outset, they fervently believed in the unity of the country. However, it became clear to Jawaharlal Nehru, Patel and others that the price of independence was the partition of the country. On 3 June, 1947, therefore, the Congress leaders signalled their acceptance of the Mountbatton Plan, whereby two new dominions were to come into existence on 15 August, 1947.[137]

In pursuance of the procedure laid down in the British Government's statement on 3 June, 1947, the two sections of the Punjab Assembly—Western and Eastern—met separately. The East Punjab section voted in favour of the partition of the Punjab by 50 to 22 votes, while the West Punjab section voted against the partition of the province by 69 to 27 votes.[138] Consequently, the Western section decided to join the new Constituent Assembly envisaged for Pakistan and the Eastern section gave their decision in favour of joining the existing Constituent Assembly for India.[139]

Once the decision to divide Punjab was taken, communal riots flared up with greater intensity in many parts of the province. The virus of communalism had infected almost every section of the society in the province, including the provincial administration and the police. Mahatma Gandhi, who had been able to control the communal frenzy in Noakhali and other parts of Bengal, did not have much influence in the Punjab. The weakness of the Congress organisation and factional fighting among its leaders discouraged him from visiting this province.[140]

It is questionable whether the partition of the country could have been avoided if the members of the Punjab Assembly had voted in favour of a United Punjab, as pointed out by

Hodson. He observes, "If Punjab through the voice of its Assembly had continued to want to remain whole, it would have been next to impossible to divide India completely."[141]

Expressing the sentiments of the people of Punjab, the Congress Working Committee said, "These tragic events have demonstrated that there can be no settlement of the problem in Punjab by violence and coercion..............Therefore it is necessary to find a way out which involves the least amount of compulsion. This would necessitate a division of the Punjab into two provinces, so that the predominantly Muslim part may be separated from the predominantly non-Muslim part".[142]

The inhuman activities which were widespread in the province were the immediate cause which forced the Congress leadership to accept the partition of the country, as expressed by Mr. J.B. Kripalani, the then Congress President, "The fear is not for the lives lost or of the widows wail or orphans cry or of many houses burnt. The fear is that if we go on like this, we shall progressively reduce ourselves to state of cannibalism and worse."[143] Thus the Congress which was against partition, accepted the plan. Even Gandhiji, who saw nothing but 'evil in the partition plan' accepted it as inevitable, because he felt the 'communal question has warped the judgement of the Congress'.[144]

The Muslim League, therefore, accepted the plan first. Thereafter, the Congress Committee passed a resolution on 15 June, 1947, accepting the proposals embodied in the announcement of June 3rd Plan. While the Boundary Commission was holding its deliberations, law and order in Punjab continued to deteriorate.[145]

After partition, there began a new era in the history of Punjab rehabilitation and resettlement after partition resulted in a significant change in the demographic pattern in the state. The East Punjab Government set up 21 refugee camps in different districts in the state and a number of such camps were also set up in the West Punjab. The refugees were to first report at the transit camps opened at the entry points like Fazilka, Ferozepur, Khemkaran, Attari, Amritsar and Dera Baba Nanak, from where they were to proceed to the areas allocated to them under the central plan.[146]

The division of Punjab on communal lines spread a sense of indignation and frustration among the Sikhs because the hope of creating Sikh State (Azad Punjab) raised by the Sikh leaders and supported by the Congress and Hindu leaders, had not been fulfilled. The Sikhs felt that they had been given a raw deal in the distribution of territory between the Hindus and the Muslims. Giving an expression to this feeling, Master Tara Singh said :[147]

> 'Every minority except the Sikhs had been given justice. The Muslim demand was Pakistan, they got it. The Scheduled Castes wanted representation on population basis with right to contest additional seats and they got it. The Sikhs demanded that they would not (like to) be dominated by any single community and they were being kicked for repeating the same demand, which the Hindus supported before partition with which the Congress sympathised.'

The Constitution, which gave a Sovereign Democratic Republic to the people of India and secured justice, liberty, equality and fraternity for the citizens, was adopted on the 26th January, 1950. The first General Elections according to its provisions were, however, held two years later in January 1952. They were based on adult franchise and the Indian National Congress swept the polls as was expected both at the Centre and in the States. In Punjab, the Congress won 97 out of 125 seats in its Legislative Assembly. Sh. Bhim Sen Sachar became the first Chief Minister of the Punjab, in the new Republic.[148]

In the beginning of 1953, two things that happened spurred the Akali Dal for greater tempo in demanding Punjabi Suba. One of them was in distant South. In 1953, Potti Sriramula died on fast for creation of Andhra Pradesh, four days later the Prime Minister announced the separation of Andhra from Madras as a Telugu-speaking State. Incidentally this spurted the Punjabi Suba Movement.[149] The Akalis were vigorously engaged in their agitation for Punjabi Suba. The States Reorganisation Commission was appointed by the Government of India on 29 December, 1953 and it was to present its report on the basis of impressions it gathered after touring different states in the country. Its members were scheduled to visit Punjab in the month of April, 1955 and the Akalis, therefore, decided to intensify their agitation. They were keen to apprise the commission with the immensity of their involvement in securing a Punjabi Suba of their concept and they organised demonstrations in several towns.[150]

Meanwhile, in October 1955, the States Reorganisation Commission issued its report in which it rejected the demand for Punjabi Suba on the ground that the problem in Punjab was not linguistic, but communal, and therefore territorial demarcation was no solution for it. On the other hand the Commission recommended the merger of Punjab, Pepsu and Himachal to create a larger territorial unit. The Akalis immediately denounced the Commission's report.[151]

The demand for a Sikh-homeland has been a perennial issue in Punjab politics ever since the pre-independence days. It has been a central theme of many political movements and controversies in the state. The demand for the Sikh-homeland was initially raised under the leadership of Master Tara Singh. The Akali Dal launched the Punjabi Suba Movement to carve out a Sikh majority state on the basis of Punjabi language. Giani Kartar Singh said that out of 14 recognised languages in the Indian Constitution, 13 states had been formed on linguistic basis, only Punjabi-speaking state had not been formed, because Sikh loyalty was suspected.[152] The Akali Dal, thus, made a common cause with the other language groups. Five member Akali delegation headed by Master Tara Singh met the Prime Minister, Maulana Abul Kalam Azad and Pandit Pant on 23 November, 1955 to represent their point of view.[153] As a result of the negotiations, a compromise formula was evolved which is known as 'Regional Formula'.

The Regional Plan was accepted by Master Tara Singh and

the Akalis, after long deliberations.[154] But it was not acceptable to the Hindu communalists and the people of Haryana. The attitude of the Punjabi Hindus dismayed the Akali party, which had welcomed the Regional Plan. The Hindi-Punjabi issue divided the people of the Punjab so sharply that it set all the political parties to revise their attitudes and policies regarding the whole problem.

Faced with the opposition from the Hindu Communal section and unwillingness of the Punjab Government to enhance the status of Punjabi language, the Akalis once again renewed the demand for Punjabi Suba. Partap Singh Kairon[155] opposed the division of the state on linguistic basis. Nehru felt that Kairon was indispensable for Punjab and got him elected in place of Sachar. Nehru believed in the saying that 'iron cuts iron'. So in practical politics, Nehru brought Kairon to crush the radical Sikh forces operating in the form of 'Punjabi Suba' agitation in the region. Kairon became Chief Minister of Punjab on 23 January, 1956.[156] Kairon was a successful leader. Kairon also had the full support of the Centre, particularly Nehru's unstained support.[157]

After suffering a setback in the elections of the executive of Shiromani Gurdwara Prabandhak Committee, Master Tara Singh outmanoeuvred his opponents and managed the merger of Akali Dal with Congress in 1956 with a view to weaken the hold of Nagoke and Majhail groups and raised the demand for Punjabi Suba within the Indian Union to outwit and defeat his political adversaries.[158]

The Regional Plan thus met with severe opposition from the Hindu sectarian groups and parties. The Government too was reluctant to implement it honestly on account of opposition from within. The Akalis, who had accepted the plan, were now faced with an awkward situation. They had to fight other challenges too. The appointment of Partap Singh Kairon as the Chief Minister and his open pro-Jat and pro-agriculturist policy threatened to wean away the few Jat members from the Akali Dal, which up to this time had its support base among the urban Sikhs.[159]

In the meantime, another Akali leader named, Sant Fateh Singh, a Jat, came to centre stage in this period of struggle. Backed by a powerful Jat peasantry, Sant Fateh Singh introduced a secular note into Akali politics by presenting the Punjabi Suba demand as based on purely linguistic consideration. The Sant declared, "We do not seek a Sikh majority area. We want the Punjabi Suba to comprise an area where Punjabi language is spoken regardless of the fact whether the Sikhs are in a majority or minority."[160]

After having failed to convince the Government by constitutional and agitational means, Sant Fateh Singh embarked on a fast-unto-death on December 18, 1960.[161] Partap Singh Kairon, the then Chief Minister of Punjab, manipulated the negotiations between Sant Fateh Singh and Jawaharlal Nehru. Sant Fateh Singh met Nehru thrice *i.e.* on February 18, March 1 and May 12, 1961, but Nehru plainly refused to approve the demand for Punjabi Suba.[162]

The rise of Sant Fateh Singh and growing resentment against Master Tara Singh to have withdrawn the fast and the movement without achieving anything, coupled with changes in the support base of Akali Dal, led to a split in the party in 1962 and transfer of leadership of the majority wing to Sant Fateh Singh. Jawaharlal Nehru, who was convinced that Punjabi Suba was a communal demand in the garb of linguistic reorganisation, took a firm decision despite a round of talks with Sant Fateh Singh. Ultimately, the Akali Dal agreed to the appointment of a Commission to go into their grievance on Government's term. But when the Commission was appointed on 31 October, the Akali Dal decided to boycott it on the alleged grounds that the names conveyed by it had not been included in the panel of the Commission.[163]

In the meantime, the third general elections were stated to be held in February, 1962. During election campaigns, Congress Sikh leaders stressed the need for communal harmony and Hindu-Sikh unity but they also emphasised, when addressing Sikh audiences that the interests of the Sikhs as a community could be better served through the Congress party than through the Akali Dal. In fact, some of them even claimed that they were Akalis. Chief Minister Kairon himself remarked at one election meeting that he was still an Akali at heart and he had left Master Tara Singh, but not the Akali Dal.[164]

Another Congress Sikh leader, running for Parliament, told an election meeting. "The Congress is bound to win in the elections, for other parties have not even put up candidates for all the constituencies. The Congress is making a Punjabi Suba, which is larger, more prosperous than the Master Tara Singh has in mind. Punjabi language will flourish more this way; more people will speak the Punjabi language. Punjabi University is being established. These are the ways to make Punjabi Suba. What has the Akali Dal done for Punjabi? They have no programme except shouting slogans for Punjabi Suba. I also am an Akali. I also went to jail in the Akali movement. Let us take the country forward. Agitations only waste resources. If there is no Hindu-Sikh unity, Punjab will be destroyed" [165] In these elections the Congress party returned to power and Partap Singh Kairon was re-elected as Chief Minister of Punjab.

During the elections for Executive of Shiromani Gurdwara Prabandhak Committee in October 1962, Master Tara Singh was dislodged from the Presidentship with a no confidence vote supported by seventy-six members. Sant Fateh Singh was elected President of SGPC in June 1963, by securing eighty-one votes against sixty-two bagged by Master Tara Singh.[166]

Meanwhile, Partap Singh Kairon's leadership came to be openly criticised by a number of legislators.[167] The death of Jawaharlal Nehru on 27 May, 1964, left Kairon without any support. After his death, the Congress became a divided house and in Punjab, the party was left without any powerful leader, who could resist the demand for a Punjabi-speaking state.[168]

The differences between Master Tara Singh and Sant Fateh Singh increased and the Akali Dal broke up into two, which was disheartening to the Akalis. Due to the Chinese aggression in 1962, Akali Dal earnestly deferred their demand. As a consequence of this the Hindu reaction to the Punjabi Suba movement was also subdued. On 16 August, 1965 Sant Fateh Singh announced plans to go to fast to be followed be self-immolation, if the Suba demand was not granted.[169] But Sant had to suspend his vow in view of the Indo-Pak war and appealed the Sikhs to unite with Hindus and help in the defence of the country.[170]

After the war, the Central Government took initiative to resolve the Punjab problem and on 9 March, the Congress Working Committee passed a resolution :[171]

> Out of the existing state of Punjab, a state with Punjabi as the state language be formed. The Government is requested to take necessary steps for the purpose.

The Punjab Boundary Commission,[172] that was set up on 23 April, 1966 to reorganise the Punjab on linguistic basis, submitted its report on the division of Punjab to the Government on 31 May, 1966. The Reorganisation of Punjab Bill was enacted by Parliament in September 1966, which came into force on November 1, 1966.

REFERENCES

1. N.V. Ramana Rao : *A Short History of the Indian National Congress,* S. Chand & Co., Delhi (1959), p. 3.
2. Tara Chand : *History of the Freedom Movement in India,* Vol. II, Publication Division, Ministry of Information and Broadcasting, Government of India, p. 549.
3. D.C. Gupta : *Indian National Movement and Constitutional Development,* Vikas Publishing House, Delhi (1970), p. 35.
4. Tara Chand : *Op. cit.,* pp. 549-50.
5. P.N. Chopra, Ram Gopal & Dr. M.L. Bhargava : *A Century of the Indian National Congress (1885-1985),* Agam Prakashan, Delhi (1986), p. 30.
6. *A Century History of Indian National Congress (1885-1985),* Vol. I, Vikas Publishing House/AICC, Delhi (1985), p. vii.
7. *Lala Muralidhar, Bakshi Tek Chand, Lala Kanehya Lal, Lala Lajpat Rai, Lala Beni Prasad, Lala Dawarka Das, Lala Dharma Dass, Sardar Man Singh, Partap Singh Sodhi, Sheikh Umar*

Batish and Muharram Ali Chisti. These are the names of some prominent delegates from Punjab, which are referred in the reports of the annual session of the Indian National Congress during 1985-1905.

8. *Proceeding of the First Indian National,* Bombay, 1885, pp. 1-2.
9. Satya M. Rai : *Legislative, Politics and Freedom Struggle in the Punjab, 1897-1947,* ICHR, Delhi, (1984), p. 19.
10. Kushwant Singh : *A History of the Sikhs (1839-1974),* Vol. II, Oxford University Press, Delhi (1977), pp. 155-56.
11. *Report of Sixteenth Indian National Congress,* Lahore (1900), p. 70.
12. Harbans Singh (ed.) : *Essays in Honour of Dr. Ganda Singh,* Patiala, (1976), p. 389.
13. H.N. Mitra (ed.) : *Indian Annual Register,* Vol. I, (1920), p. 15.
14. Pardaman Singh : *The Administration of India Under Lord Minto, 1905-1910,* (unpublished Ph.D. thesis), Punjab University, Chandigarh (1976), p. 66.
15. Partha N. Mukherjee : *"Akali and Violences"* in Amrik Singh (ed.) : *Punjab in Indian Politics : Issues and Trends,* Ajanta Publication, Delhi (1985), p. 18.
16. Azim Husain : *Fazal-i-Husain : A Political Biography,* Longmans, Green & Co., Bombay (1946), p. 77.
17. Kenneth W. Jones : *Arya Dharm : Hindu Consciousness in the Nineteenth Century in Punjab,* Delhi (1976), pp. 280-303.
18. Ravinder Kumar : *Essay in the Social History of Modern India,* Delhi (1963), pp. 47-48.
19. Azim Husain : *Op. cit.,* p. 77.
20. The General Secretaries Correspondence for the year 1918, *32nd Indian National Congress,* File No. 3, Part No. III.
21. S.L. Malhotra : *Gandhi and the Punjab,* Punjab University Chandigarh (1970), p. 5.
22. *Reports of 31st Indian National Congress,* Lucknow (1916), pp. 70-71.
23. R. Coupland : *The Indian Problem,* London (1968), pp. 61-65.
24. P. Sitaramayya : *History of the Indian National Congress,* Delhi (1969), pp. 154-63.

25. *Report of the 33rd Session of Indian National Congress,* Delhi, 1918, (1919), p. 93.
26. Syed Mohsin Shah, Sardar Sant Singh, M.S. Bhagat and J.I. Bhargava were the delegates from the Punjab to the Congress Session of 1918, *Ibid.*, Passum.
27. Raja Ram : *The Jallianwala Bagh Massacre,* Punjab University, Chandigarh (1969), pp. 38-39; also see V.N. Dutta : *Amritsar : Past & Present,* pp. 56-57.
28. "Presidential address delivered by Pt. Moti Lal Nehru on December 26, 1919." *The Indian National Congress : 34th Session,* Amritsar, (1919), Lahore, n.d. p. 10.
29. *Report of Congress Inquiry Sub-Committee,* pp. 46-47.
30. *Report of the Disorder Inquiry Committee,* p. 57.
31. *The Tribune* (Lahore), 14-15, April 1919.
32. *Report of Congress Inquiry Sub-Committee,* p. 57.
33. *The Indian National Congress, 1920-23,* pp. 27-28.
34. *Home Political,* File No. 106, July 1920.
35. *The Tribune,* October 30, 1920.
36. Ruchi Ram Sahni : *History of Our Own Times,* Vol. 4 (unpublished thesis), p. 3.
37. *The Indian National Congress, 1920-23,* pp. 28-31.
38. Feroze Chand Interview recorded by Dr. Hari Dev Sharma on January 15, 1967, Oral History Transcript, *NMML* (New Delhi), p. 37.
39. *Punjab Legislative Council Debates,* Vol. I (8 January to 16 April 1921) Lahore (1921), p. 89.
40. *The Tribune,* January 28, 1921; also see H.N. Mitra (ed.) : *I.A.R.,* (1921), p. 52(b).
41. *The Tribune,* February 1, 1921.
42. *Ibid.,* January 28, 1921.
43. *Punjab Congress,* File No. 2, 1922.
44. *Punjab Press Abstract,* January 1, 1921, Vol. XXXIV, p. 1; also see *The Tribune,* November 16, 1920.
45. *Punjab Press Abstract,* January 1, 1921, Vol. XXXIV, p. 2.
46. H.N. Mitra (ed.) : *I.A.R.* (1922), p. 60.

47. R.C. Majumdar : *History of the Freedom Movement in India,* Vol. III, Firma K.L. Mukhopadhyaya, Calcutta (1963), pp. 180-82.
48. *Punjab Congress,* File No. 2, (1922).
49. R.C. Majumdar : *Op. cit.,* p. 181.
50. *The Indian National Congress, 1920-23,* pp. 335-38.
51. K.C. Yadav : *Punjab Elections, 1920-47,* Tokyo (1981), p. 52.
52. Azim Husain : *Op. cit.,* pp. 152-53.
53. *Home Political,* File No. 138/26; also see *The Tribune,* (Lahore) 19 September, 1926.
54. *The Tribune* (Lahore), 30 October, 1926.
55. *I.A.R.,* Vol. II, (1926), pp. 70-73.
56. Satya M. Rai : *Op. cit.,* p. 144.
57. K.C. Yadav : *Op. cit.,* p. 61.
58. *Home Department,* Public, File No. 542/21.
59. M.V. Pylee : *Constitutional History of India, 1600-1950,* Bombay (1967), p. 69.
60. K.L. Tuteja : *Sikh Politics (1920-40),* Vishal Publications, Kurukshetra (1989), p. 139.
61. *The Akali Te Pardesi,* 1 and 28 January, 1928.
62. *Ibid.,* 31 January, 1928.
63. *Ibid.,* 14 March, 1928.
64. *The Tribune* (Lahore), 21 October, 1928.
65. Jawahar Lal Nehru : Autobiography, (Bombay, 1952), p. 174; also see The Tribune (Lahore), 18 November, 1928.
66. *I.A.R.* (1929) Vol. II, p. 286 also see *AICC Papers,* (1929) No. 32, *NMML.*
67. *Home Political,* File No. 15/IV, (1930) *NAI;* also see I.A.R. (1930), Vol. I, p. 34.
68. *The Tribune,* April 8, 1930, also see *Pioneer,* April 7, 1930.
69. *The Tribune,* April 8, 1930, also see *Pioneer,* April 7, 1930.
70. *AICC Papers,* (1930) No. G-32, *NMML,* also see *The Tribune,* July 31 and August 1 and 2, 1930.
71. For detail see S.C. Mittal : *Freedom Movement in Punjab, 1905-29,* New Delhi (1977).

72. *Leader,* June 28, 1930; Pioneer, June 28, 1930; *The Tribune,* June 28, 1930.
73. *Home Political,* File No. 14/28/31. *"Siapa"* was affectively used against shopkeepers in Amritsar and Lahore.
74. *The Tribune,* August 2, 1930.
75. *The Tribune,* November 5, 21 and December 1, 1930.
76. *The Tribune,* April 29, May, 1, 3, 14, 17, 20, 24
    June 10, 11-15, 17, 18, 20, 21, 24, 25, 27, 29
    July 2-13, 17, 31
    August 1, 12, 13, 14, 15, 30, 1930
77. *Home Political,* File No : 18/X, FNR of the Punjab for the first and second half of September 1930, *NAI.*
78. *Idem.*
79. *Home Political,* File No. 201/40, (1930) *NAI.*
80. *Home Political,* File No. 16/X, FNR of the Punjab for the first half of September 1930, *NAI.*
81. *Home Political,* File No. 18/X, FNR of the Punjab for the first half of September 1930, *NAI.* Also see *Punjab Administration Report, 1930-31,* p. 5.
82. *PLC,* Vol. 18, pp. 3-4.
83. D.R. Grover : *Civil Disobedience Movement in Punjab, 1930-34,* B.R. Publishing Corp. (1987), p. 147.
84. *Home Political,* File No. 5/45, (1931), *NAI.*
85. *The Tribune,* January 28, 1931.
86. *Home Political,* File No. 18/3/1931, FNR of the Punjab for the first half of March 1931, *NAI,* also see *I.A.R.* (1931) Vol. I, pp. 26-28.
87. *I.A.R.* (1931), Vol. II, p. 33.
88. *Leader,* April 13, 1933.
89. D.R. Grover : *Op. cit.,* pp. 293-94.
90. *The Tribune,* April 22, 1935.
91. K.L. Tuteja : *Op. cit.,* p. 175.
92. V.P. Menon : *Transfer of Power in India,* Orient Longmans, Delhi (1957), p. 54.

93. *Indian National Congress, 1934-36,* pp. 77-78.
94. *The Tribune,* June 9, 1935.
95. *AICC,* File No. E-17/1937; also see *The Tribune,* June 9, 1936.
96. *Home Political,* File No : 4/9/1937, *NAI.*
97. S. Gopal (ed.) : *Selected Works of Jawaharlal Nehru,* Vol. III. (1965), pp. 383-85.
98. *AICC,* File No. G-31/1936, *NMML.*
99. Statement of Gopi Chand Bhargava, *The Tribune,* November 18, 1936.
100. *AICC,* File No. E-17/1937, *NMML.*
101. Statement of Gopi Chand Bhargava, *The Tribune,* November 20, 1936.
102. File No. 20/111/36-F, Reform Office, *NAI.*
103. *Ibid.*
104. *The Tribune,* March 7, 1937.
105. *The Tribune,* March 3, 1937.
106. Hira Singh Dard : *Panth : Dharma Te Rajneeti,* Jullundur, n.d., p. 43.
107. Master Tara Singh : *Meri Yaad,* Amritsar, 1945, p. 126.
108. Durlab Singh : *The Valiant Fighter : A Biographical Sketch of Master Tara Singh,* Lahore (1942), pp. 123-24.
109. Kamlesh Sharma : *Role of Muslims in Indian Politics, 1857-1947,* New Delhi, p. 209.
110. *The Tribune's* Files, May-October 1937.
111. S. Gopal (ed.) : *Op. cit.,* p. 301.
112. Craig Baxter : *The 1937 Elections and the Sikander-Jinnah Pact in the Punjab : Past and Present,* Vol. X-II, Patiala (1976), p. 370.
113. V.V. Nagarkar : *Genesis of Pakistan,* New Delhi (1975), p. 320.
114. *I.A.R.* Vol. I, (1940), pp. 228-29.
115. *Ibid.,* pp. 268-72.
116. V.V. Nagarkar : *Op. cit.,* p. 322.
117. Harbans Singh : *The Heritage of the Sikhs,* New York (1964), p. 178.
118. Fortnightly Report for Punjab for the second half of April 1940, *Home Political,* File No. 18-4-90 : Poll (I).

119. Harbans Singh : *Op. cit.,* p. 271.
120. B.R. Nanda : *Mahatma Gandhi : A Biography,* George Allen Unwin Ltd., London (1958), p. 456.
121. Harbans Singh : *Op. cit.,* p. 271.
122. *I.A.R.* Vol. II, (1942), pp. 209-11, *Congress Handbook,* New Delhi (1946), pp. 265-69.
123. A Centenary History of the Indian National Congress (1885-1985) : *Op. cit.,* p. XXIX.
124. *Ibid.*
125. *Ibid.*
126. *Home Political,* File No : 3/16/1942, Poll (I) Part-I.
127. A.C. Arora (ed.) : *Punjab Dian Lok Lehran, 1847-1947,* Patiala (1989), p. 117.
128. Satya M. Rai : *Op. cit.,* p. 287.
129. K.C. Gulati : *The Akalis : Past & Present,* New Delhi (1974), pp. 118-119.
130. Khushwant Singh : *A History of the Sikhs, 1839-1974,* Oxford University Press, Oxford (1966), p. 259.
131. Kshitish : *Storm in Punjab,* New Delhi (1985), p. 104.
132. *I.A.R.,* Vol. I, (1946), p. 205.
133. B.R. Nayyar : *Minority Politics in Punjab,* Princeton University, Princeton (1966), p. 93.
134. A Centenary History of the Indian National Congress (1885-1985) : *Op. cit.,* pp. XXX-XXXI.
135. *Ibid.*
136. Khushwant Singh : *Op. cit.,* p. 273.
137. A Centenary History of the Indian National Congress (1885-1985) : *Op. cit.,* p. XXXI.
138. *I.A.R.* (1947) Vol. I, p. 112(c).
139. Satya M. Rai : *Op. cit.,* p. 329.
140. *Ibid.,* pp. 329-30.
141. H.V. Hodson : *"The Role of Mountbatten"* Paper Presented at the Study Conference on the Partition of India, July 1967, (unpublished).
142. H.V. Hodson : *The Great Divide,* London (1969), p. 242.

143. F. Tuker : *While Memory Serves,* London (1950), p. 257 quoted in Satya M. Rai : *Punjab Heroic Tradition,* 1900-1947, Publication Bureau, Punjabi University, Patiala (1995), pp. 173-74.

144. Pyare Lal : *Mahatma Gandhi : The Last Phase,* Vol. II, Ahmedabad (1958), p. 322.

145. Khushwant Singh : *Op. Cit.,* p. 278.

146. Satya M. Rai : *Punjab Since Partition,* Durga Publication, Delhi (1986), p. 110.

147. *Ibid.,* p. 249.

148. Pt. Mohan Lal : *Disintegration of Punjab,* Sameer Parkashan, Chandigarh (1984), p. 1.

149. Krishan Gopal : *Dynamics of Punjabi Suba Movement,* Deep and Deep Publications Pvt. Ltd., New Delhi (1999), p. 70.

150. Pt. Mohan Lal : *Op. cit.,* p. 21.

151. B.R. Nayer : *Op. cit.,* p. 245.

152. *Akali* (Punjabi), 14 October, 1955.

153. *The Hindustan Times,* 24 November, 1955.

154. *The Tribune,* 16 March, 1956.

155. *The President of Punjab State Congress.*

156. Krishan Gopal : *Op. Cit.,* p. 224.

157. S.C. Arora : *Turmoil in Punjab Politics,* Mittal Publishers, New Delhi (1990), p. 58.

158. Dalip Singh : *Dynamics of Punjab Politics,* McMillan, New Delhi (1981), pp. 225-26.

159. Satya M. Rai : *Op. Cit.,* p. 304.

160. *The Tribune,* 30 October, 1960.

161. Sant Fateh Singh : *Abhul Yaadan,* Ganganagar (1962), p. 19.

162. *The Tribune,* 13 May, 1961.

163. Satya M. Rai : *Op. cit.,* pp. 306-07.

164. Speech at Village Dholan in Jagraon Assembly Constituency, Ludhiana, February 13, 1962.

165. From Field notes, speech delivered in Punjabi, quoted in B.R. Nayar : *Op. cit.,* pp. 304-05.

166. J.S. Garewal : *The New Cambridge History of India : The Sikhs of Punjab,* Orient Longman, New Delhi (1990), p. 200.

167. Pt. Mohan Lal : *Op. cit.*, p. 207.
168. Karishan Gopal : *Op. cit.*, p. 232.
169. Iqbal Narain (ed.) : *State Politics in India,* Meenakshi Prakashan, Meerut (1976), p. 265.
170. Rajinder Kaur : *Sikh Identity and National Integration,* Intellectual Publishing House, New Delhi (1992), p. 60.
171. *The Hindustan Times,* 10 March, 1966.
172. The Punjab Boundary Commission comprise three members :
    1. *Justice Jayanti Lal Chhota Lal Shah,* Judge of Supreme Court.
    2. *Sh. Subi Mal Dutt,* A Former Secretary.
    3. *Sh. M.M. Philip,* Secretary, Ministry of Transport and Communications.

3

Mountbatton to Mountbatten

After the announcement of the Mountbatten plan on the 3rd June, 1947, for the division of the country into India and Pakistan on the basis of religion, the Boundary Commission was appointed under Sir Cyril Redcliffe to demarcate the areas into Muslim and non-Muslim. The partition of Punjab shook the administrative, economical and political machinery of the province to its foundations and brought into its wake a host of complicated problems. The problems were so interlinked that aggravation of one complicated the other, although it is difficult to say whether the situation of one tangle could lead to the unknotting of the other.[1]

The present Punjab is, in part, the result of the 1947 partition. As in case of Bengal, the partition resulted in the division of the province of Punjab, splitting into two parts, the 'Land of Five Rivers', which had been referred to as, "the shield, spear and sword hand of India."[2] The partition constitutes a traumatic watershed in the politics of the truncated state of the Punjab, which came to India's share. Since 1947, the state has been variously known as the Indian Punjab, East Punjab and Punjab (India) but is now referred to as simply the Punjab.[3]

Scattered across the map of Punjab, the States of Patiala, Jind, Nabha, Kapurthala, Faridkot, Nalagarh, Malerkotla and Kalsia, later on constituted the Patiala and East Punjab States Union (PEPSU). These territories owed their existence to no difference in character between their people or territories and those of the British Punjab. The territories of these States were dovetailed into and closely interwoven with those of British Punjab.[4]

Meanwhile, the negotiations among the Princes over the future of the East Punjab States had also begun. The rulers of Patiala, Jind, Nabha, Kapurthala, Malerkotla and Kalsia convinced themselves that it was no longer possible for the States to continue as independent units for the people were on the war-path, administration in these States was crisis-ridden and the Central Government at Delhi, which was under the Congress, was not sympathetic. In such a situation, the movement for merger of these states gained ground. A non-official poll taken by the Jind State Praja Mandal in Jind and Charkhi Dadri showed that people there overwhelmingly wanted merger with the East Punjab.[5] In Kapurthala State, where, there were three pockets of Kapurthala, Phagwara and Bhunga and in the Kalsia State, the movement for merger with East Punjab was also quite strong.[6]

By the time the Government of India took stock of the political situation in East Punjab and in the Punjab States, the demand for the amalgamation of the Punjab States and the new State of Himachal Pardesh with East Punjab gathered momentum among the nationalist Sikhs. The Central Government thought of four alternatives : first, amalgamating Himachal Pardesh and the East Punjab States with East Punjab leaving out Patiala, which had been declared a viable unit;[7] second, amalgamating Patiala and Himachal Pardesh with the East Punjab States; third, amalgamating the States of Kapurthala, Jind, Nabha, Malerkotla and Faridkot into a single unit leaving out Himachal and Patiala and fourth, integrating all the East Punjab States including Patiala into one union.[8] Sardar Patel expressed his opinion that in the existing circumstances, the East Punjab province, Himachal Pradesh and East Punjab State should be kept as three separate units.[9]

The Maharaja of Faridkot supported by some Akali Sikh leaders toyed with the idea of a union of Faridkot, Jind, Kapurthala and Nabha excluding Patiala, in the hope that he would be enabled to play an important role in the Sikh politics of the Union.[10] But Udham Singh Nagoke, a nationalist Sikh leader firmly opposed this move. He was not in favour of any union, which did not include Patiala. He strongly pleaded for a separate union of the East Punjab States.[11]

As is evident from the correspondence between the Nawab of Malerkotla and the Maharaja of Patiala, the former lustfully yearned for his own personal possessions and comforts. In a subsequent letter, the Nawab wrote that there could be no better solution than to have union with Patiala on the basis of an accession on the subjects of Legislature, Defence, External Affairs and Communications. He proposed an agreement between the State of Patiala and the States of Nabha, Jind, Malerkotla and Faridkot.[12]

In one of his letters to the Government of India, the Maharaja of Kapurthala urged the immediate necessity of the formation of a union of the four states—Jind, Kapurthala Faridkot and Nabha—as a preliminary step in view of the circumstances prevalent in the country.[13] But in a subsequent meeting with Mountbatten on 10th February, 1948, he urged that it would be in the interest of all the Punjab States if a union of all the States including Patiala was formed.[14] Similarly, the Maharaja of Jind in his letter of 7th April, 1948, wrote to the Maharaja of Patiala that "the East Punjab States cannot usefully form a union amongst themselves until and unless Patiala is agreeable to such an arrangement."[15]

On the question of associating Patiala with the East Punjab States Union, the Government of India was of the opinion that there should be a union of all the East Punjab States and as a Patiala state was capable of standing by itself, it should be left alone. In a communication of 10th March, 1948 to the Maharaja of Patiala, Patel assured that he was keenly interested as before in the Patiala State maintaining its legitimate position.[16] The Government at first gave an option to Patiala on a voluntary basis to join any arrangements for a union of the East Punjab States.[17]

In the course of his talk with the Central Government, the Maharaja at number of times had talked about the desirability of canalizing Sikh politics in response to which he was assured of the establishment of a separate union of the Punjab States so as to satisfy the aspiration of the Sikh community.[18]

While giving due importance to the Patiala State and its ruler, the Government of India did not accept the Maharaja's request to confer a hereditary Rajpramukhship on the house of Patiala. He was, however, appointed Rajpramukh of the Union for life, whereas the Maharaja of Kapurthala was made Uprajpramukh. It was decided that the Union would be called the Patiala and East Punjab States Union (PEPSU) till such time as the Constituent Assembly of the Union should adopt a more suitable title.[19] On 5th May, 1948, the Rulers of all the eight States signed the covenant. The Pepsu was inaugurated on 15th July, 1948, but it actually came into political existence on 20th August, 1948, when the Rajpramukh took over the administration of the covenanting States.[20]

Inaugurating the new Union of Patiala and East Punjab States, later known as Pepsu, on 15th July, 1948, Sardar Patel characterised it as a "Homeland of the Sikhs". The Pepsu enjoyed financial and political viability and had 1, 721, 935 Sikhs as against 1, 704, 339 Hindu and 55,913 Muslims inhabiting it according to 1951 census.[21] Description of the new State as Sikh Homeland was later utilised by the Akalis as a argument in favour of retention of the Pepsu and Master Tara Singh, who welcomed its formation time and again advocated the merger of the Sikh majority areas of Punjab into the Pepsu and formation of a Punjabi-speaking State.[22]

Rejection of the Praja Mandal demand for merger and acceptance of the Akali proposal for the formation of the Patiala and East Punjab States Union once again proved that the Congress High Command did not consider the Praja Mandal as the sole spokesman of the people of these States. It rather attached more importance to the Akalis and the viewpoint of the Princes. With the formation of Pepsu, the Praja Mandal also changed its name to the Pepsu Pradesh Congress and became a direct unit of the Indian National Congress.[23]

The formation of Patiala and East Punjab States Union was

the first phase in the process of fitting the erstwhile Princely States into the structure of India. An important development that followed the formation of Pepsu was the execution of fresh Instrument of Accession on behalf of the Union. Prior to this, the individual States joining the Pepsu had acceded to Indian Dominion in respect of three subjects only, namely, Defence, External Affairs and Communications. The Rajpramukh, in accordance with the provision made in the covenant signed a fresh Instrument of Accession[24] on 6th May, 1948. Thus the State of Pepsu was ensured of the constitutional uniformity with other provinces of the Indian Dominion.[25]

However, neither Mountbatten's plan nor Punjab Assembly's decision to divide the Province put an end to the ongoing communal orgy; the period from June to August was full of communal murders, arson and looting. The communal virus tore apart the centuries old cultural and social ties of the Punjabi society. On both the Indian and Pakistan sides, horrible atrocities were committed. Foot-weary convoys of refugees were attacked till the roads were clogged with corpses; trains were attacked and sent across the borders with bogies packed with slaughtered passengers. Even sick or the aged or infants were not spared by the communal frenzy on the both sides. The fear of death persisted in the mind of every migrating person. Never in the history of the world was there a bigger exchange of populations attended with so much bloodshed.[26] "There must be many examples in the bloody history of mankind where the extent of violence had been as great or even greater, but it is probably true that there has never been such a huge exchange of population," says Horace Alexander.[27]

According the Stephen P. Landas, in the Convention of La-Usanne 1923, between Greece and Turkey both "caused the up-rooting of two million people."[28] But in the case of the East Punjab and West Punjab, more than eight million people crossed the border. The exchange of the population between Turkey and Greece, hitherto known as the biggest of its kind was accomplished in a year or so, whereas in the East Punjab and the West Punjab the transfer of eight million people was completed in three months.[29]

After the partition of India in 1947, half a million non-Muslim refugees poured into East Punjab States. Their rehabilitation at different places in the Pepsu was the biggest problem faced by the Government immediately after the formation of Patiala and East Punjab States Union. The phenomenon of forced mass transfer of population had implications of a political, social and economic character. The refugees had been the victims of remorseless plunder, rape and arson. They brought with them nothing, but bitter memories of loss and sufferings. They came to strange towns and villages by all conceivable means—trains, military lorries, and bullock carts in long trailing carvans and even on foot. The Pepsu Government was yet to be on its legs, when the administration of the covenanting States had to find an answer to the problems of relief and rehabilitation.[30]

The State of Patiala was the first to receive the refugees early in the year 1947.[31] In response to Maharaja Yadvinder Singh's offer to give an asylum, some 50,000 refugees came to Patiala between March and July 1947.[32] The Faridkot State offered to rehabilitate 40,000 refugees in addition to the 20,000 who had come over to the State before 15 August, 1947. The state of Nabha offered to provide relief to 50,000 refugees. In the Kapurthala State, refugee camps were opened at Kapurthala, Phagwara and Sultanpur Lodhi.[33] For the purpose of coordination among the States, and with the East Punjab Government, a conference was held at Jullundhar on 3rd December, 1947. As a result of its deliberations, steps were taken which resulted in the establishment of Rehabilitation Council for East Punjab and East Punjab States under the Chairmanship of a Minister of Central Government.[34]

The Pepsu Government in order to settle the displaced persons, set up the Relief and Rehabilitation Secretariat at Patiala in 1948. The separate Directorates, one for the rural rehabilitation and other for the urban rehabilitation, were established.[35] In all the districts, Assistant Directors and Assistant Commissioners of Rehabilitation were appointed.[36]

The idea of group allotment or equal distribution

"frightened many people". Some thought it to be a "collectivist experiment".[37] In this situation, the Congress party committed to abolition of landlordism and to establish socialism, could have taken effective steps. The CPI in its memorandum to the East Punjab Government urged that the rehabilitation policy must be "based on democratic foundations and fitted into the general task of building up a democratic agrarian economy and reconstruction". They demanded that it would be in consonance with programme of abolition of landlordism and distribution of land among tillers of the soil.[38]

There could obviously be no agreement between the small and big refugee landholders on the pattern of land allotment on account of the clash of interests of the two groups. Yielding to the pressure of the big landlords, the Government evolved a policy of 'graded cuts'.[39]

On the persistent demand of the displaced landholders, urgent considerations were given to the questions relating to the permanent allotment of land. Keeping in view the small quantity of land available and to satisfy the prevalent sentiments among refugees, who held land in West Punjab, it was announce that the land would be allotted only to those who, in the West Punjab were owners, occupancy tenants under the Punjab Tenancy Act and tenants under the Colonizing of Government Land Act.[40] The final scheme of allotment of land was based on the following principles :[41]

1. *Only owners of land in West Punjab were given land in Pepsu.*
2. *A system of graded cuts was applied while making allotments.*
3. *Lands left by Hindus and Sikhs in West Punjab and evacuee land in Pepsu was converted into standard acres.*
4. *Special provision for urban lands, gardens and sub-urban lands were made.*
5. *Persons only from certain areas in West Pakistan were given lands in Pepsu.*

6. *Allotment was made in the form of lease without rent for three years.*

The Government while distributing land among the displaced persons had to take into consideration the restoration and reconstruction of rural economy. The land resettlement process was not an easy task. The officials and the staff concerned worked day and night before the displaced persons could be resettled, but a good number were still left dissatisfied because a large area of evacuee land had been grabbed either by influential local people or displaced persons.[42] These charges were not denied by Director of Rehabilitation.[43] It is alleged that the staff in charge of the recovery of looted property sent their own men to loot the houses before they made a list of the property therein.[44]

Various political parties gave suggestions regarding the policy to be followed for the resettlement of the refugees. The Refugee Conference, Jan Sangh and the Akali party wanted the displaced persons should be given full compensation on the basis of property left in Pakistan. The Communist party stressed that the whole land should be pooled and distributed equally among the displaced landholders and landless tillers.[45]

The first and the immediate need of the displaced persons, after food and temporary housing in camps, was to have residential accommodation. Acute shortage of houses made it imperative for the government to immediately take up the issue of repairing Muslim evacuee houses. The Government was very slow in sanctioning in repairs in the beginning, but later the work was expedited to meet the requirements of the displaced persons. The evacuee houses, however, were not sufficient to accommodate all the displaced families.[46] The Pepsu Government also decided to establish some sub-urban colonies and model townships in some of its towns for the refugees.[47]

The number of houses left behind by the Muslims in the rural areas was 1.56 lacs. Out of this 1.10 lacs houses were allotted to the displaced persons.[48] Of these 62,000 were allotted to refugees before January 1951 and another 31,000 were given soon after repairs.[49] The rest of them were so badly damaged that they could not be allotted to the refugees.

By the year 1950-51 out of 5 lac displaced persons, who had come over to Pepsu nearly 1.90 lacs were from urban areas. Housing of refugees was the major problem on account of a number of reasons. First, the number of urban refugees was far more than the number of urban Muslims, who migrated to West Pakistan, secondly, most of the evacuee houses were not equipped; with necessary amenities of life like water and electricity.[50]

To start with, the construction of houses proceeded at a "snail's pace," but it made considerable progress subsequently and 3640 houses were completed by the end of the December 1948. The government also decided to sell these build-up houses as well as building sites in the colonies to the refugees to speed up construction work. Besides, it worked out a plan to give loans, repayable in easy instalments to the refugee buyers for purchase of sites and building the houses.[51]

The Gopalaswami Ayyanger Committee, had been appointed by the Ministry of Rehabilitation, Government of India, to review rehabilitation work, recommend a rehabilitation plan within the available resources, submitted its scheme for the year 1950-51. The Committee estimated that one-lac houses would be required for people uprooted from West Pakistan alone. This meant that nearly Rs. 50 crore were required for the purpose of house-building.[52]

The Pepsu Government also decided to establish some sub-urban colonies and model townships in some of its towns.[53] A Middle Income Group Housing scheme was initiated by the Government for the construction of houses. Aid under this scheme was given to those, whose income did not exceed Rs. 5000 per annum and the maximum ceiling on the advance to an individual was fixed at Rs. 8000.[54] A sum of 10.97 lac rupees was sanctioned for construction of houses in Model Town, Patiala.[55] An amount of Rs. 2.54 lacs was advanced for the construction of a residential complex near Gurdwara Dukhniwaran, Patiala. In Tripuri township of Patiala, an approximate amount of Rs. 13 Lacs were spent and 1100 houses were built.[56] 960 quarters were constructed in the other parts of Patiala, Nabha and Sangrur at a cost of Rs. 15 lacs.[57] By the year 1954, the Pepsu Government spent a sum of Rs. 18 lacs for the construction of houses. Out of 770 houses constructed with this amount 520 were in Patiala, 170 at Nabha and 80 at Sangrur.[58]

After the first requirement of residential accommodation for the displaced persons was met, the next important step was towards effecting speedy rehabilitation in their avocations. According to a laid down policy, the evacuee shops and factories were only allotted to the displaced persons. The only essential conditions of eligibility was that the displaced persons, who claimed allotment of a shop or factory, had carried on similar business or industry in the West Punjab.[59] There were in all 1,885 allottable shops; 241 shops were demolished, while 2448 were habitable and 206 repairable.[60] To help refugees settle in small scale business, 126 shops were constructed in Patiala at a cost of Rs. 1.72 lacs.[61]

The newly formed State of Pepsu faced a great upheaval during the initial period of its existence. A study of this period reveals that the lawless elements had made the task of rehabilitation of refugees more difficult. But despite this the Pepsu Government had solved the problems of rehabilitation with great measures of success because the Central Government under the Congress leadership with its vastly, superior resources, mature guidance and leadership came to the rescue of the newly formed Union. The Central Government withstood all the jerks and enabled the infant State to face the arduous task of rehabilitation of the refugees.[62]

After the initial trauma, the refugees positioned themselves into a state of complete self-support. They hated charity, but were anxious to stand on their own legs. Soon they began calling themselves 'purusharthi' and hated to be called 'sharnarthi'.[63]

Formation of a Government in the Pepsu gave a little headache to the political parties. There were three distinct claimants for power the Praja Mandal, the Akali Dal and the Communist Party. Before the formation of the Pepsu, the Congress had been supporting the Praja Mandal from outside. Consequent on the merger of All India States People Conference with the Indian National Congress in May, 1948, the Praja Mandal in the East Punjab States merged itself with the Congress. The new party came to be known as Pepsu Pradesh Congress.[64]

However, the States Ministry proposed to install a coalition ministry of the representatives of the Praja Mandal, the Akali Dal and the Lok Sewak Sabha. As no agreement could be reached among the three claimants, the Union came into existence with Maharaja Yadvinder Singh of Patiala as Rajpramukh.[65] Efforts continued for the formation of a representative ministry, but the resistance offered by the Akalis and the erstwhile Praja Mandalists to Rarewala or Raghubir Singh's leadership was too strong to overcome. Ultimately, a ministry of Lok Sewak Sabha and four rebel Praja Mandal representatives, Giani Zail Singh, Ram Nath, Nihal Singh Takshak and Harcharan Singh under Gian Singh Rarewala was sworn in on 13 January, 1949.[66] This ministry was set up by the Rajpramukh after informal consultations with Patel.[67]

The interim ministry came under heavy attack from the Akalis and pro-Brish Bhan Congressites. Gian Singh Rarewala, being a close relative of the Maharaja of Patiala, the Akalis dubbed it as a "Mama-Bhanja Wazart", (a ministry of maternal uncle and his nephew). Ministers were greeted with black flags wherever they went. Section 144 had to be imposed to protect ministers from Akali demonstrators. The holding of political meetings and demonstrations and the shouting of slogans were prohibited.[68] Forty Congress workers were prosecuted and sentenced to various terms of imprisonment.[69] In the face of stiff Akali-Praja Mandal opposition, the new ministry could not last long.[70] On 18 November, 1949, the Pepsu's so called 'broad-based ministry' was dissolved. After two days, the Government of India installed the second caretaker government, which consisted Gian Singh Rarewala and M.R. Bhide, an I.C.S. officer. This caretaker government lasted nearly one and a half year. Though not of a popular character, it succeeded in improving the law and order situation.[71]

It was soon replaced by a purely Congress Ministry under Col. Raghubir Singh, who joined Congress after dissolving his Lok Sewak Sabha. The ministry assumed office on 23rd May, 1951 and included Brish Bhan as Deputy Chief Minister and three of his nominees as Ministers as also two of his Harijan supporters as Deputy Ministers.[72] But this was no victory for Brish Bhan as he had to accept Col. Raghubir Singh as his chief and share power with Giani Zail Singh and Nihal Singh Takshak, whom the official Pepsu Congress (Praja Mandal) had been condemning as traitors. It is interesting to note that between July 1948 and May 1951, the Pepsu witnessed four interim ministries, three of which were formed under Gian Singh Rarewala and one under Col. Raghubir Singh.[73]

The first General Elections in 1952 were fought by three parties; the Akali Dal who had been ignored throughout in ministry formation; the Pepsu Congress with the new converts under Col. Raghubir Singh and the Communist party. The Pepsu being a part—B State, its legislature had only sixty seats. The 1952 elections brought into bold relief the main weaknesses of Pepsu politics in general and the Praja Mandal in particular. Central leadership of the Congress had already taken steps for broadening the organisation by bringing Col. Raghubir Singh's group into the state Congress and forcing Brish Bhan to accept his leadership.[74]

The election results showed that the Congress had only a limited appeal. Out of sixty seats contested by it, it could win hardly twenty-six seats while the Akalis captured nineteen and the Communists three.[75] The rest were taken by independents and smaller parties. Taken region wise, the Congress performance was better in the Hindi-speaking area, where it won nine out of the fourteen seats. In the main Punjabi-speaking districts, where it was facing an organised opposition from the Akalis, it had to concede them the first position. Out of a total of forty-four seats, the Congress could win only seventeen, whereas the Akalis and Independents supported by them captured twenty one.[76]

Table 3.1. Results of 1952 Elections in Pepsu

S. No.	*Party*	*Seats won*
1.	Congress	26
2.	Akali Dal	19
3.	Communists	3
4.	Kisan Mazdoor Praja Party	1
5.	Jan Sangh	3
6.	Scheduled Castes Fedration	1
7.	Independents	7

The Congress formed the Government under Col. Raghubir Singh as Chief Minister with the help of the independents. But it fell shortly as its nominee for Speakership was defeated by one of its own Deputy Ministers. The speaker had been defeated in dramatic circumstances. However, he was adopted as candidate by the newly formed United Front comprising Akalis, anti-Congress elements and independents led by Gian Singh Rarewala.[77] The non-Congress ministry with Rarewala as its head was formed on 21 April, 1952, with the help of the legislators from the Hindi-speaking zone.[78]

The Rarewala ministry remained in office for about a year, but throughout its existence, it ever remained under threat of defection by over-ambitious legislators particularly from the Hindi-speaking region. The conditional support of three Community MLA's and faction fights among the Akalis did not allow the Rarewala ministry to function smoothly.[79] It fell in March 1953 and President's rule was proclaimed.[80] The resignation of Rarewala's ministry on 1 March, 1953 climaxed a phase of bewildering political developments. In the following one-year of President's rule (1953-54) in the state, some significant changes were witnessed in the behaviour pattern and character of the political parties.[81]

The Congress during the year of President's rule had patched up the growing cracks within its organisation. It mobilised the Central leadership for its propaganda. The Prime Minister of India-cum-Congress President, Central Ministers and Chief Ministers of Punjab, Himachal and Rajasthan visited the Pepsu. The difference among the Congressmen were resolved and the organisation was revitalized. The leaders of Pepsu Congress applied their energies and efforts in setting their houses in order and in educating the masses. The administration in Pepsu also helped "to prop up the withering Congress organisation in the state."[82] The feudal elements saw the wisdom of making friends with the Congress soon after the meeting held between Nehru and Rajpramukh.[83] The Congress welcomed the inclusion of the representatives of Sikh landed aristocracy in its organisation. It appeared that the Congress had been guided by the twin consideration of weakening the Akalis and giving representation to the Sikh community on a broader basis than hitherto.[84]

Of all the political parties in Pepsu, the Congress faced the election of 1954 with full confidence. In the conduct of election campaign, the Pepsu Congressmen showed a solidarity, which surprised all those who were aware of the serious nature of their differences and jealousies in the past. Another factor that gave the Congressmen boosted confidence was the national character of the Congress party. The Congress also had the advantage that it was a well-knit unit and was in power at the Centre. Many former rulers offered their hands of cooperation to the Congress. They badly wanted to rehabilitate themselves psychologically in the new set-up and also sought an opportunity to serve the country.[85]

In the election of 1952, the Congress had secured over 3.95 lac votes[86] out of the total polled votes of 10.52 lacs and bagged 26 seats, but in the 1954 elections, they got total of 6.96 lac (43%) of votes and captured 37 seats.[87] The Akalis who had emerged as the second largest party in the first elections, at the time of second elections were a bitterly divided house. The Communists had come out of the second

General Elections more powerful. They had improved upon their strength as compared to the last assembly elections both in quality and quantity.[88]

Table 3.2. Party Position in the 1954 Mid Term Polls in the Pepsu

S. No.	*Party*	*Seats Won*
1.	Congress	37
2.	Akali-cum-National Front	14
3.	Sanjha Morcha and the Communists	7
4.	Others	2

It was for the first time that a single political party (Congress) with a clear majority was elected. In Pepsu, the victory of Congress ended the political uncertainty in a vital border state. On 6th March, 1954, Col. Raghubir Singh, President of Pepsu Congress, was elected unanimously as the leader of the Pepsu Congress Assembly Party. On 8th March, he was sworn in as the Chief Minister along with Brish Bhan as a Cabinet Minister. The Pepsu's Cabinet was a fairly representative one from the point of view of Congressmen. Raja Surinder Singh of Nalagarh elected from the hilly district of Kandaghat, represented the Princely order. General Shivdev Singh, former Chief Minister of the erstwhile State of Nabha, represented big landholders and leading families. Col. Raghubir Singh represented the interests of the local erstwhile Patiala State. Prem Singh Prem represented the interests of the displaced persons from West Pakistan and Harcharan Singh, an advocate from Bhatinda, represented Giani Zail Singh's group in the Congress.[88]

The non-Congress critics objected to the over-representation of feudal interests and went to the extent of describing the cabinet as a "palace show".[90] The Congress party consisted of heterogeneous elements, some had no political past, others had opposed the Congress more than they had worked for it. The 'old timers' were mostly former Praja Mandlists, who thought their alliance with the feudal order was temporary. Most of the members remained ignorant of the Five-Year Plan report and the ideological basis of Congress politics.[91]

By the middle of July 1954, the Congress organisation was divided on the issue of merger of Pepsu with Punjab, into two groups—one, comprising members of the former Praja Mandal led by Brish Bhan favouring the merger and the other of the old, Lok Sewak Sabha Party under Col. Raghubir Singh opposing the merger. The Congress, which was the ruling party in Pepsu, did not enunciate a clear policy. Most of the Pepsu Congressmen wanted Pepsu to be merged into Punjab, but the Punjab Congressmen by and large, did not favour such a proposal as they apprehended that it would involves the surrendered of their Hindi-speaking areas, where they had the maximum mass appeal.[92]

On 29 December, 1953, the Parliament appointed the States Reorganisation Commission (hereafter given as SRC) to examine 'objectively and dispassionately' the question of the reorganisation of the states of the Indian Union as that the welfare of the people of each constituent unit as well as the nation as a whole be promoted.[93]

As regards the Congress stand, the picture got radically changed after the death of Col. Raghubir Singh on 7 January, 1955. The group of Congressmen who had been loyal to him was greatly weekend. In the absence of Col. Raghubir Singh, no eminent Congressman supported the "retention of Pepsu as a separate unit."[94] Soon after Brish Bhan's taking over as the Chief Minsiter of Pepsu, a piquant situation arose because he was known to have pro-merger views which ran counter to the stand taken by the Pepsu Government in the Memorandum submitted to the SRC in 1954.[95]

The Working Committee of All Indian Congress Committee in its meeting in April 1954, decided that all Congress Committees and Congressmen should have full freedom to represent their points of view before the States Reorganisation Commission.[96] In case of any difference of opinion, the minority in any Congress Committee was free to represent its views before the Commission. The Punjab Congress Committee, accordingly, decided that Congress members would meet the SRC in their individual capacity. It is an open secret that majority of Hindu Congressmen advocated merger of Himachal and Pepsu in the Punjab, while a larger number of Sikh Congressmen supported the demand of the Punjabi-speaking province.[97]

Almost all the political parties and other organisations met the SRC on 18 April, 1955 at Patiala. The Akali delegation, the Communist Party, the deputation of Ganganagar Citizens, the Bhatinda District Citizens Committee and the Barnala Citizens Committee demanded the creation of a Punjabi-speaking state.[98] The Akalis in Pepsu pleaded for the retention of Pepsu, preferably in an expanded or modified form. Three groups—the Arya Samaj, the Krishak Samiti and the Central Pursharthi Sabha—demanded the merger of the Pepsu with the Himachal and the Punjab.[99]

The SRC after considering various proposals and requests gave its recommendation on 30th September, 1955. In its report, the SRC maintained that both physically and geographically; Pepsu was very much a party of the Punjab. From the point of view of population, Pepsu was the smallest of Part-B states. The demand for its merger as a whole or by parts in the adjoining areas had been voiced by the political parties right from the time of its formation till the appointment of SRC. The SRC argued that PEPSU was an artificial unit and could not continue under any scheme of reorganisation. The Commission said :[100]

> We feel that even with its present territory, the state cannot be regarded as a sizeable unit and with the merger outlying pockets in the adjoining areas which should follow as a natural corollary of territorial readjustments in this area, it will become very difficult for this state to maintain its separate existence.

The SRC argued that it would be simpler and more economical, besides being conductive to more efficient administration, if the states were merged. The alternative to this proposition, as voiced by the various political parties, was the creation of either a Punjabi-speaking state or Maha Punjab. The SRC strongly felt that both of these demands were communal because they were intended to tilt the balance in favour of one or the other of the two main communities.[101]

The Congress party viewed the recommendations of the SRC favourably and managed a unanimous resolution. It hailed the liquidation of Pepsu, pleaded for the recognition over the abolition of the institution of Rajpramukh.[102] The Communist Party of India strongly opposed the anti-merger movement launched jointly by a section of the Akali Dal and the landlords in the Congress Party. It described the recommendation of the SRC on the dissolution at Pepsu as a 'partial victory' for the anti-feudal struggle of the people.[103]

While merging Pepsu with Punjab on 1st November, 1956, the Government of India had to sort out the problems regarding the abolition of the institution of the Rajpramukh. The SRC did not go into the question of the commitments, which the Government of India had made to the ex-rulers of the Princely States. Consequently, the institution of the Rajpramukh was abolished.[104]

In the Pepsu, it was widely felt that if as a result of reorganisation of state boundaries, Pepsu ceased to be a separate state unit, Patiala should be made the capital of the new Punjab State. As a sop to the extremists sentiments, specially among the Sikhs, the Congress Party backed the demand for the location of the capital at Patiala.[105] But the ultimate decision did not go in favour of Patiala City, but in accordance with the recommendations of the SRC,[106] it was decided to retain some important government offices in Patiala. The Central Government decided that Chandigarh would be the capital of the new Punjab.

Sensing the feelings of the masses of the Pepsu and realising the incongruities inherent in this unit, the States Reorganisation Commission gave its verdict in favour of the Pepsu's merger with the Punjab. Consequently, the Pepsu was made an integral part of the Punjab on 1 November, 1956.[107]

REFERENCES

1. Satya M. Rai : *Punjab Since Partition,* Durga Publications, Delhi (1986), p. 243.
2. Reginald Coupland : *The Indian Problem : Report on the Constitutional Problem in India,* Oxford University Press, New York (1944), Part I, p. 116.
3. B.R. Nayar : *Minority Politics in Punjab,* Princeton University Press, Princeton (1966), p. 11.
4. Gursharan Singh : *History of PEPSU,* Konark Publishers Pvt. Ltd., Delhi (1991), p. 1.
5. *The Hindustan Time,* 29 March, 1948.
6. *Ijlas-i-Khas,* S. No. 2040, B. No. 25/171, Future of East Punjab States, PSR, p. 19 (*PSA*).
7. V.P. Menon : *The Story of the Integration of Indian States,* Bombay (1956), p. 243.
8. *The Free Nation,* Ambala, Vol. I, No. I, 19 November, 1948, p. 4.
9. V.P. Menon : *Op. cit.,* p. 243.
10. *Ibid.,* p. 241.
11. Durga Das (ed.) : *Sardar Patel's Correspondence, 1945-50,* Vol. IV, Ahmedabad (1972), pp. 324-26.
12. *Ijlas-i-Khas,* S. No. 2042, B. No. 25/171, P. 43PSR, *(PSA), AISPC* Papers, List No : 3, File no : 108, p. 7, *(NMML).*
13. *Ijlas-i-Khas,* S. No. 2040, B. No. 25/171, Future of the East Punjab States, p. 13, PSR *(PSA).*
14. *Ibid.,* p. 19.
15. *Ijlas-i-Khas,* S. No. 2042, B. No. 25/171, Future of the East Punjab States, p. 13, PSR *(PSA).*
16. *Ijlas-i-Khas,* S. No. 2040, B. No. 25/171, Future of the East Punjab States, p. 17, PSR *(PSA).*
17. *Ibid.*
18. *The Tribune,* 19 July, 1959; also see *The Indian News Chronicle,* 26 April, 1948.
19. V.P. Menon : *Op. cit.,* pp. 245-46.
20. Gursharan Singh : *Op. cit.,* p. 55.
21. *Facts About Pepsu :* Patiala : Directorate of Information and Public Relations, Pepsu, 15 July, 1953.

22. *Hindustan Time,* Delhi, 2 June, 1948.
23. Ramesh Walia : *Praja Mandal Movement in East Punjab States,* Punjabi University, Patiala (1972), p. 191.
24. Gursharan Singh : *Op. cit.,* pp. 264-65.
25. *WPIS*: p. 24.
26. Khushwant Singh : *A History of the Sikhs (1839-1974),* Vol. II, Oxford University Press, Bombay (1965), p. 282.
27. Horace Alexander : *New Citizens of India,* Oxford University Press, p. 7, quoted in Kirpal Singh : *The Partition in Punjab,* Publication Bureau, Punjabi University, Patiala (1972), p. 140.
28. Stephan P. Landas : *The Exchange of Minorities,* New York (1932), p. 3.
29. *Millions on the Move,* Publication Division, Government of India, Delhi (1948), p. 10.
30. Gursharan Singh : *Op. cit.,* p. 77.
31. Mohan Singh : *Report on the Working of Relief* (Patiala), p. 5.
32. *Ibid.,* pp. 6-7, Camps were opened at Bhatinda, Dhuri, Barnala, Sanour, Samana, Mansa, Raman, Lehragaga and Narwana.
33. *Millions on the Move,* pp. 62-63.
34. L.R. Nair (ed.) : *Rural Rehabilitation in East Punjab, 1947-48,* Simla, (1948), pp. 22-24.
35. *The Times of India,* 16 July, 1953; also see J. Nanda : *Punjab Uprooted,* Bombay (1948), pp. 70-71.
36. *Ibid.,* also see Satya M. Rai : *Partition of Punjab,* New Delhi (1963), p. 123.
37. *The Statesman,* 25 July, 1950.
38. *Communist Party Documents,* Memorandum, 22 December, 1947.
39. Gursharan Singh : *Op. cit.,* p. 287.
40. M.S. Randhawa : *Out of Ashes,* Punjab (1954), p. 70.
41. M.R. Bhide : *Progress of Rehabilitation in Pepsu,* Patiala (1951), p. 31.
42. Satya M. Rai : *Op. cit.,* p. 167.
43. Interview with *Tarlok Singh,* Director General, Rural Rehabilitation, East Punjab, by *Master Hari Singh,* 3rd January, 1948.

44. Satya M. Rai : *Op. cit.*, p. 168.
45. *C.P.I. Documents*, No. 10/40, 3rd February, 1948.
46. Satya M. Rai : *Op. cit.*, pp. 171-72.
47. *PVS*, Vol. VII, No. 2, 20 July, 1955, pp. 177-78.
48. *The Tribune*, 6 August, 1954.
49. *PLA*, Vol. IV, No. 2, 9 July, 1954, p. 130.
50. V.P. Malhotra : *Economic Conditions of Displace Persons Settled in East Punjab*, Part-I, Ludhiana (1949), pp. 11-12.
51. Satya M. Rai : *Op. cit.*, p. 172.
52. *Ibid.*, p. 173.
53. *PVS*, Vol. IV, No : 1, 22 February, 1955, p. 7, Model Towns were planned in Patiala and Phagwara for the rehabilitation of refugees.
54. *PVS*, Vol. VI No. 12, 14 March, 1955, pp. 222-23.
55. *PVS*, Vol. VI No. 14, 11 March, 1955, p. 1107.
56. Supplements to *The Hindustan Times*, 22 September, 1955.
57. *Ibid.*
58. *The Times of India*, 10 September, 1954.
59. *Relief and Rehabilitation in Punjab*, p. 24.
60. M.R. Bhide : *Op. cit.*, p. 40.
61. *Pepsu Since Inauguration*, p. 38.
62. Gursharan Singh : *Op. cit.*, p. 107.
63. *The Punjab Past and Present*, Vol. XX-II, October 1986, Department of Punjab Historical Studies, Punjabi University, Patiala, p. 387.
64. Teja Singh Nidharak : *Mockery With Democracy*, Simla (1948), p. 1, Resolution Passed by Praja Mandal Conference, 19 June, 1948, List No. 3, File No. 133, p. 1, *AISPC* Papers (*NMML*).
65. V.P. Menon : *Op. cit.*, pp. 248-49.
66. *The Statesman*, 15 July, 1955.
67. *Ministry of States*, Letter No. 1098P/V, File No. 3(85), p. 494 *(NAI)*.
68. Deputy Commissioner, Fatehgarh's Order, 24 April, 1949, Vide *Pepsu Government Gazette Extraordinary*, 1 May, 1949 (Patiala) *(PSA)*.

69. Tara Chand Gupta : *Nine Months of Popular Ministry in Pepsu, Congressmen, What's Now?* Patiala (1949).
70. Ramesh Walia : *Op. cit.*, p. 104.
71. Gursharan Singh : *Op. cit.*, p. 124.
72. *Historical Background of Pepsu,* A State Government's Publication, 1952.
73. Ramesh Walia : *Op. cit.*, p. 194.
74. *Ibid.*, p. 195.
75. Analysis of election results based on information provided by India, 1953, Published by the Publication Bureau, Government of India, New Delhi.
76. Ramesh Walia : *Op. cit.*, p. 196.
77. *The Tribune* and *The Hindustan Times,* 21 March, 1952.
78. Manju Verma : *The Coalition Ministries in Punjab,* Patiala (1978), p. 28.
79. 'Pepsu Inquiry', *The Delhi Express,* 30 January, 1953.
80. Ramesh Walia : *Op. cit.*, p. 197.
81. Gursharan Singh : *Op. cit.*, p. 131.
82. *The Times of India,* 4 October, 1953.
83. *The Hindustan Times,* 6 December, 1953.
84. Gursharan Singh : *Op. Cit.*, p. 135.
85. *The Tribune,* 13 February, 1954, *The Times of India,* 16 February, 1954.
86. *The Hindustan Standard,* 11 February, 1954.
87. *The Tribune,* 10 March, 1954.
88. *Ibid.*, 16 March, 1954.
89. *The Times of India,* 19 May, 1954.
90. *Ibid.*, also see *The Statesman,* 17 May, 1954.
91. Gursharan Singh : *Op. cit.*, p. 145.
92. *The Statesman,* 17 November, 1954.
93. Resolution of the Government of India, Ministry of Home Affairs, File No : 53/69/53 : Public, 29 December, 1953.
94. *The Times of India,* 8 June 1954 & 19 April, 1955.
95. *The Hindustan Times,* 24 April, 1955.

96. *Resolution of States Reorganisation, 1920-56,* A Publication of *AICC,* (New Delhi), p. 8.
97. Satya M. Rai : *Op. cit.,* pp. 290-91.
98. *The Tribune,* 19 April, 1954.
99. *Ibid.*
100. *State Reorganisation Commission,* p. 148.
101. *Ibid.*
102. *The Hindustan Times,* 11 October, 1955.
103. *The Times of India,* 14 October, 1955, *The Tribune,* 20 October, 1955.
104. Gursharan Singh : *Op. cit.,* p. 240.
105. 'Location of Capital for Greater Punjab', *The Hindustan Times,* 3 December, 1955.
106. *States Reorganisation Commission,* p. 149; also see *The Times of India,* 31 December, 1955.
107. Gursharan Singh : *Op. cit.,* p. 254.

4

Relation Among Various Political Parties

The partition not only brought changes in the social composition of the society, but also in the political configuration of the State of Punjab. With the large-scale migration of Muslims from the Punjab, the Muslim League ceased to be a political force in the state. The Unionist Party had become redundant before the partition and attempts to revive it later in the Haryana region ended in failure. The Congress party emerged as the strongest political force and assumed political power in the Punjab after the partition.[1]

The Congress party as an all India party occupies a unique position in the Indian political system. All three levels of the political system—government, regime and political community—are identified with it and are, in part, its handiwork. Except for a few short periods in a couple of states, the Congress party had remained firmly in control of the government, both at the Centre and in the state, since independence in 1947. As a broad-based secular party, encompassing all kinds of social and political groups, the Congress party was the standard bearer of secularism and nationalism. During the struggle for independence, it identified and equated itself with what it considered to be the Indian nation. It claimed to be the sole representative of the entire Indian nation. When independence was finally achieved, the Indian people generally accepted the Congress party's claim that it was the architect of Indian freedom; the party was recognised as the creator of free India, the Indian nation or the Indian political community. Subsequent to the achievement of independence, the new constitution of India, with the secular state and parliamentary democracy as its corner stones, was formulated under the leadership of the Congress party. The new constitutional system, the regime—was recognised as the embodiment of the aims, aspirations and the ideals of the Congress.[2]

Apart from the Congress, there were three other organised political parties of major significance on the political scene in the Punjab : the *Shiromani Akali Dal*, the *Bhartiya Jan Sangh* and the Communist party. Except the *Akali Dal*, the other two parties were all India political parties, although the strength of the *Jan Sangh* and the Communist party had been due to their strong hold in certain regions of India. In contrast, the Akali Dal was a regional party and only confined to the Punjab. Moreover, its rank and file belonged only to the Sikhs. As a regional party, it stood for watching the interests of Sikh community. The *Akali Dal*, by and large, opposed the Congress party on a number of issues.[3]

The Jan Sangh despite its protestations to the contrary, was a Hindu communal party, which considered the existing regime as not in harmony with Indian tradition. Its aim was suspected to be that of establishing Hindu supremacy in India. As for the Communist party, it was feared that it would inevitably try to establish totalitarian regime if it ever came to power by absolute majority. In the case of Punjab, the Communist party was by and large a Sikh party, both in terms of its membership and leadership.[4]

When the Congress party launched its own non-cooperation movement against the British Government in 1920's, the Akali movement began to be considered a part of it although the specific purpose of the *Akali* movement was to bring their shrines under the control of Sikh community. A reciprocal relationship thus developed between the two movements; the *Akali* movement became a part of the nationalist movement and, in return, received the blessings of the Congress leadership in its objectives. As a result of this association in the early 1920's, the *Akali Dal*, which emerged as a para-military political organisation during the Akali movement, although careful to maintain its separate organisation continued to lend support to the Congress party in the freedom movement against the British Empire. At the same time, the Akali Dal functioned as a pressure group for the Sikh community in relation to the Congress party : for instance, it opposed the report of the Nehru Committee because the party considered it not particularly advantageous for the Sikhs. For its part, the Congress party, while receiving support from the Akali Dal, aggregated and channelled Sikh demands as part of the nationalist demands.[5]

In 1929, at its session in Lahore, the Indian National Congress acceded to the demand that it should not agree to a constitution, which was not acceptable to the Sikh community. While cooperating with the Congress party, the *Akali Dal* engaged independently in political activity to secure political privileges specifically for the Sikh Community.[6]

During the 1930's, the Communal Award continued to dominate Indian politics. The Muslims felt reassured by the special rights and concessions it gave them. The Hindus were naturally hostile. In view of the divergence of opinion between the two communities, the Congress adopted an attitude of discreet neutrality. At a meeting in Bombay in October 1934, it neither accepted nor rejected the Award. The Sikhs considered the Award a menace to their existence. They were its bitterest opponents and did not slacken their campaign against it. But they were numerically too few for their protest to have much effect. The British Parliament approved the Award by enacting the Government of India Act of 1935.[7]

After the elections of 1937, which the *Akali Dal* contested as a separate political group, the *Dal* aligned itself more closely with the Congress party and even asked its members to join the Congress. Many of its functionaries came to occupy important positions in the Congress organization. It is alleged that the Akali Dal joined the Congress at this time in order to use the Congress party machinery for its own purpose. In November 1938, the Akali's held an All India Akali Conference at Rawalpindi under the Presidentship of Baldev Singh. Akali and Congress flags were flown side by side. The conference expressed lack of confidence in the Unionist Government because of its repressive measures and exhorted the Sikhs to join the Congress, the only representative political organisation in the country.[8] Be that as it may, the Akali Party's policy, first of co-operation and then of collaboration with the Congress continued until 1939, when differences began to develop and the Dal moved away from the Congress.[9]

In March 1940, the Muslim League passed a resolution demanding a sovereign Muslim State that would comprise the predominantly Muslim areas of India including most of the Punjab. The Sikhs were deeply disturbed by this demand. The only alternatives for the Sikhs were either to align themselves with the Indian National Congress and resist the Muslim demand for the partition of India or to strive for a state of their own.[10]

The Sikhs found themselves in a tricky situation. They were faced with two rival freedom movements; one led by the Indian National Congress for freedom of country as a whole; the other led by the Muslim League for an independent Muslim State involving a division of the country which would inevitably cut across the land in which the Sikhs lived.[11]

The Sikhs began to pin their faith in the Congress because Congressites ranging from Mahatma Gandhi down to the humblest volunteer had sworn that they would never suffer the dismemberment of the country. The Indian National Congress climaxed its obduracy by launching in August 1942, a campaign to force the English to "Quit India". Mahatma Gandhi and all the leading Congressmen were arrested. The Congress party was declared illegal. Punjab remained peaceful; the arrest of Congressmen went practically unnoticed.[12]

On May 7, 1945, Nazi Germany laid down arms. The Government of India felt the time had come to make another attempt to win over Indian politicians to its side. Congress leaders were released. The events that took place in 1947 were, thus, an outcome of the developments that had made their headway in the last hundred years (1849-1947). The importance of the Punjab as nucleus of the demand of the Muslim League for Pakistan made it the hot-bed of all types of political intrigues.[13]

In January 1946, elections to the Punjab Legislative Assembly were held. The party position in the 175 member Punjab Assembly after the election was :[14]

Table 4.1. Punjab Legislative Assembly Elections, 1946

S. No.	*Party*	*Seats won*
1.	Congress	51 (Hindus-40 including 4-SC, Muslim-1, Sikh-10)
2.	Muslim League	74
3.	Unionist	21 (Muslim-12, Hindu-2, Harijan-3, Christian-1)
4.	Akalis	23
5.	Anglo-Indians	2
6.	Independent Christian	1
7.	Independent Labour	2
8.	Independent Harijan	1

The Muslim League came out as not only the largest Muslim party but also the single largest party in Punjab Assembly. It could not however form a ministry unless it joined with some other party. The Congress and Akalis formed a working alliance and a coalition ministry, consisting of Congress, Akali and Unionist party, under the leadership of Malik Khizar Hayat Khan.[15] The Muslim League, which was determined to establish 'undiluted Muslim rule' over Punjab, felt very sore and therefore, directed all its energies towards overthrowing the coalition ministry.[16]

Meanwhile, the Labour Prime Minister, Mr. Atlee, announced that a team of cabinet ministers would visit India to discuss the next step towards Indian independence.[17] But finding that the Cabinet Mission plan had proved unworkable, Prime Minister Atlee, sent Lord Louis Mountbatten as Viceroy to India in early 1947 to attempt a solution of the Indian crisis. After negotiations over a period of a few months, the leaders of the Congress party, the Muslim League and the Akali Dal agreed through an announcement in the first week of June 1947, to the Mountbatten Plan for the partition of the country and the formation on August 15, 1947 of the two dominions—India and Pakistan.[18]

On August 15, 1947, as India celebrated its independence, nearly ten million Punjabis were at each other's throats. In East Punjab, the Muslim police were disbanded and the Muslims were left to the mercy of marauding bands of Sikhs and R.S.S. militia. Sikh violence attained its peak in September 1947.[19]

The East Punjab Government was organised with a temporary capital at Shimla. Sir Chandu Lal Trivedi was appointed Governor. Gopi Chand Bhargava was elected Chief Minister by the legislators who came over to the Indian side.[20] Bhargava included in his ministry representatives from the Nagoke group of the Akali Dal, which was known for its pro-Congress sympathies in the pre-independence period. However, the Congress legislature party was about equally divided between two factions with a long history—the Satyapal group and the Bhargava group—and the Bhargava's position was quite precarious.[21]

A few week later, Akali leaders met in New Delhi and directed the Akali members of the Punjab legislature to resign from the Akali Dal and join the Congress party.[22] The Akali Dal's decision to join the Congress party was interpreted by some as a victory for secular nationalism as the Akali Dal had decided to give up its separate 'communal' politics, but in fact the decision was 'actuated by the desire to assure continuance of the existing ledership'.[23] The Akali members inside the Congress party functioned as a separate group under the leadership and direction of Giani Kartar Singh and Bhargava became increasingly dependent on the support of this group to maintain his position as Chief Minsiter.[24]

In April 1948, Punjab was declared bilingual province with both Punjabi in Gurmukhi and Hindi in Devnagri script as its languages. But the educationists proved to be as susceptible to political and religious pressure as the politician. The Hindu members constituted a majority in the Punjab University Senate and when the Sikh members discovered that their demand could not be met, they walked out of its meeting in protest. The Hindu members adopted a resolution embodying their point of view, which in the absence of the support of the representatives of the other community was not considered a workable solution. Consequently, the Punjab Government decided to take the initiative in the matter.[25] The Punjab Government submitted its proposals popularly known as "Sachar Formula"[26] on the language question on 1 October, 1949.

The Formula was widely acclaimed by the Sikhs including the Akalis, though they criticized the right of the parents to choose the medium of instruction for the education of their children.[27] The proposals, however, met with severe criticism at the hands of the Hindu organisations like the Arya Samaj, the Jan Sangh and the Hindu Mahasabha. In order to counter the Akali demand of the Punjabi Suba and the claim of Punjabi as the regional language of the Punjabi-speaking area, these organisations and the Hindi vernacular press started a campaign that the Hindu of this area should declare Hindi as their mother-tongue.[28]

The Jan Sangh, the Arya Samaj as well as most of the Hindu Congressmen in Punjab, notably Lala Jagat Narain, who was the General Secretary of the Punjab Pradesh Congress Committee and owned a chain of vernacular newspapers based at Jullundhar, launched a vigorous campaign in the press and from door to door, urging the Hindus to get Hindi recorded as their mother-tongue. The whole atmosphere was surcharged with communal poison and in the month of February, 1951, a number of communal riots took place in various towns.[29]

On the other hand, the Akali members in the Congress had 'skilfully used their bargaining power to precipitate crisis between rival Hindu leaders in the Congress party or to reap the maximum advantage out of the crisis when it occurred.'[30] Bhargava now included Giani Kartar Singh in his ministry. In return for Akali support, Bhargava had to yield, "all along the line to importunate demands" to the Akali group.[31] The leadership of the Congress organisation strongly criticized the Congress government headed by Bhargava. Partap Singh Kairon attacked the Bhargava ministry for including persons "who were directly responsible for the communal bitterness that existed in the province today".[32] He remarked, "some of them were active and bitter opponents of Congress. They joined the Congress only when they realised that the only way to get into the power was through the Congress".[33] Finally, the Central Congress leadership in New Delhi reacted by directing Bhargava to resign and then imposed 'President's Rule' in the Punjab in 1951 on the ground that the constitutional machinery had broken down in the state. The legislature was dissolved and the Governor of Punjab administrated the state until the first general elections in 1951-52.[34]

The First General Elections under the new constitution were held in 1951-52. There is no doubt that the elections in 1952 were fought on the basis of the Punjabi Suba demand in the background.

But the Akali Dal was badly mauled by the Congress in this election both in Punjab and Pepsu. In the final outcome, the Akali Dal was having only 33 out of 186 legislative seats (126 in Punjab and 60 in Pepsu). On the other hand, Congress percentage in non-Sikh majority districts went below 21.7%. The Akali Dal failed to muster the support it had expected and could not substantiate its claim to be the sole representative of the Sikhs.[35]

Table 4.2. Percentage of Seats and Votes Polled by Political Parties in 1952 (Punjab and Pepsu)

S. No.	*Political Party*	*Total Seats in Vidhan Sabha*	*% of Votes*
	(Punjab and Pepsu)		
1.	Congress	122	34.8
2.	Akali Dal	33	14.7
3.	Communist Party	06	5.3
4.	Jan Sangh	06	5.0
5.	Others and Independents	21	40.2

Source : Compiled from Indian Election Commission, *Report on the First General Elections in India, 1951-52,* Vol. II, New Delhi, 1955.

On 22nd November 1953, the States Reorganisation Commission was appointed. Five days after this announcement, Prime Minister Nehru was on a visit to Pepsu at the invitation of the Rajparmukh. His only engagement in the state was to address a congregation in the main hall of Gurdwara Fatehgarh Sahib. Master Tara Singh had arrived there at the head of a strong contingent with the avowed object of gagging him. Accordingly, no sooner did Nehru rose to speak than the Master was on his feet and started haranguing interminably, despite expostulations of the Rajparmukh with the result that Nehru left the hall without having his say. He had never before had such an experience.[36]

Within a week of this extraordinary incident, Nehru was back in Pepsu. This time he had come to open the Congress campaign at the mid-term election to the state assembly of 1954. When addressing a public meeting at Patiala, he had another brush with the followers of Master Tara Singh, who were shouting themselves hoarse that they would not rest content until they had secured a Punjabi Suba. Angered with their demonstration, Nehru uttered the warning that he would not allow any further division of the country. The Congress swept the polls.[37] The Congress assumed power in Pepsu with Col. Raghubir Singh as premier and Brish Bhan as his deputy.[38]

The climate in Punjab was charged with excitement following the appointment of State Reorganisation Commission. The Akali Dal submitted a memorandum urging the formation of a Punjabi-speaking state. It claimed all the districts of Jullundhar division with the exception of Kangra, the entire Pepsu, large portions of Ambala division and Ganganagar district of Rajasthan.[39]

The Maha Punjab Samiti, in its memorandum, advocated its demand of Maha Punjab, comprising of Punjab, Pepsu, Himachal, Delhi and few western districts of the United Province. They held that this was more suitable in the changed political situation of this border state after the partition. Consideration of unity and security of India must outweigh all other considerations, they argued. The strategically geographic situation of Punjab demanded that the state should be strong enough "to face the aggressive and hostile challenges of Pakistan".[40]

The Communist Party, in its memorandum to the S.R.C. put up a strong case for the Punjabi-speaking province, which was in line with their all India policy of reorganisation of the Indian territory on linguistic basis. They, however, emphasised their difference with the Akali Party with regard to the basis for this demand and inclusion of certain territories in the proposed new state. In view of this, the party recommended that Pepsu State should be dissolved and merged in Punjab, but the Hindi-speaking areas of Punjab and Pepsu should be made into a separate Haryana or Hindi-speaking state. The Communist party was of the opinion that the hilly districts of Kandaghat of Pepsu and Kulu in Kangra district should be joined with Himachal Pardesh. The Praja Socialist Party and other socialists also supported the formation of states on linguistic basis.[41]

The Jan Sangh submitted its memorandum for Maha Punjab to the States Reorganisation Commission emphasising that for greater and more intensive development of the national resources of this region, and to serve the best interests of the people inhabiting this area, and in order to convert this region into a defence wall of the north-west border of the Union of India, the integration of East Punjab, Pepsu and Himachal into a single administrative organisation was strategic necessity of the first magnitude.[42]

The Jan Sangh memorandum described the Akali demand for a Punjabi-speaking state as similar to the Muslim League demand for the division of the country in the pre-partition days. In a resolution the Jan Sangh denounced the creation of Punjabi-speaking state as politically undesirable, physically impossible, linguistically and economically untenable and normally unjustifiable.[43]

The States Reorganisation Commission which visited Punjab in April 1954, went into the question of Punjabi Suba very minutely. The Working Committee of All Indian Congress decided in April 1954 that all the Congress Committees and Congressmen should have freedom to represent their point of view before the S.R.C.[44] The Congress party supported the demand for the enlarged Punjab. The Punjab Government also advocated the formation of a greater Punjab comprising Punjab, Pepsu, Himachal, Delhi and few districts of U.P.[45]

The States Recognisation Commission submitted its report in October 1955. It rejected the demand for Punjabi Suba and recommended the merger of Punjab, Pepsu and Himachal Pradesh. Executive Committee of the Punjab Pradesh Congress Committee welcomed the report.[46]

The Akali Dal denounced the Commission's report and threatened to launch an agitation. At last parlys were held between the Government and the Akali Dal. These resulted in an agreement between the two, which is called the 'Regional Formula'.[47] Under the Regional Formula, the state was divided into two regions called Punjabi-speaking and Hindi-speaking regions.

The Government of India empowered the state government to demarcate the Hindi and Punjabi regions. The regional language of each region was declared as the official language. With a view to promote the development of the two languages—Hindi and Punjabi—it recommended establishment of two separate departments. It recommended that 'Sachar Formula' should continue to operate in Punjab State.[48]

The Regional Plan was accepted by Master Tara Singh and the Akalis after long deliberations. In a press statement on 15 March, 1956, explaining the reason for the acceptance of the plan, Master said that the scheme fulfilled the aspirations of the Sikhs to an extent and at the same time did not give them any opportunity to dominate others, a power if given might result in making them 'undemocratic and narrow-minded.'[49]

Regional Plan, however, was not acceptable to the Hindu Communists and the people of Haryana. The Maha Punjabis were opposed to the suggestion of Hindi being made a second language in the proposed Punjabi region and accused the government of yielding to the Akali pressure. In a conference held at Karnal on 25 June, 1956, it resolved, "in the considered opinion of this conference the Scheme for Regional Standing Committees is no solution of the Punjab problem and is also no solution of the peculiar problem (backwardness of the area) of Haryana."[50]

The Akali Dal had not yet reached any decision, when Gian Singh Rarewala, a former Chief Minister of Pepsu, who had been called the "Panzer Division" of the Akali Dal,[51] issued a statement in May 1956 urging that, under the changed circumstances, the Akali Dal should leave the political field and confine itself to only social, cultural, religious and educational activities of the Sikhs.[52] He wanted the Akali Dal to allow its members and supporters "to join the progressive and national forces and take full part in the rebuilding of the country."[53] He later started discussions with Congress leaders in order to facilitate the entry into the Congress party of his group, which was especially strong in the former Pepsu area. Master Tara Singh immediately branded Rarewala's move as a 'treachery' and made it clear that the Akali Dal would maintain its independent existence, because of his belief in the independent political entity of the Sikhs.[54]

Finally, the executive committee of the Akali Dal expelled Rarewala and four of his prominent supporters from the Akali Dal for their endeavour to join the Congress party.[55] The strong criticism of Rarewala was made not because of his advice to join the Congress party but because he openly advocated it.[56]

It was not long after the Rarewala group joined the Congress party that the Akali Dal started negotiations with Congress leaders about political cooperation. In October 1956, it decided through a resolution that the Akali Dal 'would in future concentrate and confine itself to religious, educational, cultural, social and economic betterment of the Sikhs' and that 'in regard to political activities the members and supporters of the Akali Dal would be advised to join' the Congress party.[57]

After some hesitation the Akali constitution was amended

in accordance with the wishes of the Congress party. Most of the prominent Akali leaders and their supporters joined the Congress party, but Tara Singh decided to stay out.[58] It was playing Hamlet without the Prince. The Master chose to keep his options open after signing his pact with Nehru on dotted lines.[59]

The country was now on the eve of its Second General Elections. The Central Congress Election Committee, which has the last word on the choice of party candidates, was screening the Punjab list. After much bargaining, the Congress party eventually established a quota of 26 seats for the Akali Dal.[60] The announcement of the final list of nominees provoked a revolt. Master Tara singh was the first rebel against his own pact with Nehru. In order to redress the balance, he nominated another 22 Akali candidates in his individual capacity to oppose the official Congress nominees.[61]

In the general elections of 1957, none of the Panthic nominees of Tara Singh succeeded however, whereas the Congress party had 120 seats in the house of 154. Among the newly elected legislators, 22 were elected on the Akali quota and about 6 belonged to the Rarewala group.[62]

In the 1957 general elections, the Congress polled more votes in the assembly elections, than it had done in 1952. During the 1952 elections, the Congress party had firmly opposed the demand for Punjabi Suba and had been able to win considerable Hindu and Harijan votes. Prior to the 1957 general elections, the Congress party conceded the regional formula to the Akali Dal and had witnessed the Dal to merge politically into the Congress Party. In this manner, it was able to secure larger support from the part of the Sikh community, which was under the influence of the Akali Dal, but in the process it also lost a large part of the Hindu votes.[63]

Table 4.3

Party-wise Position in the Punjab Assembly Election, 1957[64]

Total Votes Polled	73,51,164
Invalid Votes	1,67,334
Valid Votes	71,83,830
Percentage of Votes Polled	53.76%

	Party	Seats Contested	Seats Won	% of Votes Polled
1.	Congress	154	120	47.51
2.	Communists	69	6	13.56
3.	Praja Socialist	15	1	1.25
4.	Jan Sangh	64	9	8.60
5.	Scheduled Castes Federation	24	5	5.39
6.	Socialists (Lohia)	8	0	0.49
7.	Independents	115	13	23.20
	Total	**449**	**154**	**100.00**

The analysis of election results reveal that there were significant shifts in the support bases of different political parties. There was a unique shift in the urban Hindu support from the Congress in 1952 to the Jan Singh in 1957. A section of Hindus, both rural and urban supported the Jan Sangh. Since the Akalis did not participate in the elections, the rural Sikhs supported the Congress, whereas the urban Sikhs opted for the independents and Jan Sangh. The Communist party of India got a good number of votes from the rural areas.[65]

After the assembly elections, Partap Singh Kairon was elected as the leader of the Congress assembly party on 3rd April, 1957. He formed the Congress Ministry and inducted two erstwhile Akalis Gian Singh Rarewala and Giani Kartar Singh in his Cabinet. Kairon took control of both the Congress party organisation and the government transforming bi-factional cleavage into single group dominance.[66]

The Akali Dal's daily 'Jathedar' observed in October, 1961 that if the regional formula had been implemented in the spirit in which it had been conceived by the Central leadership under the guidance of Jawaharlal Nehru, then no further trouble would have arisen in Punjab.[67]

On September 16th, 1958, Master Tara Singh announced that the regional formula in Punjab had not been satisfactorily implemented and he said, "I will be compelled to reopen the demand for Punjabi Suba".[68] After Master Tara Singh's declaration to attain Punjabi Suba, the entire Punjab Government machinery was moved to oust him from the Presidentship of the Shiromani Gurdwara Parbandhak Committee. Giani Kartar Singh vehemently supported Prem Singh Lallpura against Master Tara Singh. Master Tara Singh was defeated by three votes because Giani Kartar Singh got the support of all the 24 Communists and 3 Congress members.[69]

No doubt, Master Tara Singh had been defeated and a nominee of the Congress Ministry had been installed as the President of the S.G.P.C., but it was apprehended in Congress circles that Master Tara Singh would be able to regain his position, unless measures were taken to keep him out of power in the S.G.P.C. The second Punjabi Suba Conference was held at Chandigarh. Master Tara Singh addressed a mammoth gathering of more than 25,000 persons, the first of its kind in the then capital of Punjab, wherein he reiterated the demand for Punjabi Suba and said that he was contemplating holding a mass movement on a scale compared to which all previous agitation would pale into insignificance. Master Tara Singh did not lose the opportunity and announced that he would take out a silent procession of the Sikhs in Delhi to demonstrate that the Sikhs wanted to register their protest against the interference of the Government in the Gurdwara administration and he fixed March 15,1959 for the purpose. But Master Tara Singh was arrested on March 13, 1959 at midnight.[70]

A silent procession was taken out, estimated to be between 50,000 to 3 lacs by different reporters of the newspapers, starting from the Parade Ground at 11 a.m. A huge All India Dharmik Conference was held in the lawns of Rakab Ganj Gurdwara, where a resolution was passed expressing great resentment at the arrest of Master Tara Singh and declaring it 'wholly unwarranted'. Master Tara Singh was released on 21 May, 1959 presumably on the intervention of Centre.[71]

Knowing that no agitation would succeed as long as Kairon was in power, the Akali Dal first turned its attention to dislodge him from his position of Chief Ministership. In this it was unsuccessful, however, the Akali Dal then pressed even more stridently for Punjabi Suba and also started a campaign against alleged government interference in the Gurdwaras. Meanwhile, the Gurdwara elections were approaching and the Akali Dal spent much of 1959 in organising its election campaign.[72]

The 1960 elections of the Shiromani Gurdwara Prabandhak Committee turned out to be another trial of strength between the Congress and the Akalis. Congress Sikhs led by Partap Singh Kairon and Giani Kartar Singh, strove hard to defeat Master Tara Singh and his nominees. Giani Kartar Singh resigned from the cabinet to apply all his energies to electioneering. With the overt help of the state government, he sponsored a society called 'Sadh Sangat Board' to contest the elections. But the results went overwhelmingly in favour of the Shiromani Akali Dal. The Dal took 136 seats contrasting with 'Sadh Sangat Board's' four. All the Akali members assembled at the Akal Takhat on June 24, 1960 to bind themselves solemnly to achieve Punjabi Suba.[73]

In April 1960, Master Tara Singh resigned from his position as S.G.P.C. President in order to devote himself entirely to the movement for Punjabi Suba. In the same month the Akali Dal decided to call a convention of various political parties that supported its demand for Punjabi Suba.[74] The convention was attended by a large number of people including many Hindus and Muslims, members of the Swatantra Party, Praja Socialist Party and Samyukta Socialist Party workers and leaders.[75] The main resolution was moved by Justice Gurnam Singh, which was supported by other urging upon the country and the Government of India "not to delay any more the inevitable formation of the state, when all other linguistic states have already been carved on linguistic basis."[76]

The Akali Dal now decided to organise a 'Shahidi Jatha', which would start from the Akal Takhat at Amritsar under

Master Tara Singh's leadership and leisurely moving through the Punjab, reach Delhi in about two weeks to head a passive procession.[77] Convinced that the Akalis were about to launch a morcha and unlike the government under Sachar, eager to retain the initiative in such a contest, the Punjab Government under Kairon proceeded to arrest Master Tara Singh under the Preventive Detention Act on account of his 'indulging in such activities so as to arouse religious sentiments of the Sikhs against Hindus'. The government deemed such a step necessary in order "to save the state from getting into a chaotic condition and with a view to maintaining peaceful relations between the two communities". Simultaneously, the government made large-scale arrests of other Akali leaders and workers and also imposed several restrictions on the press.[78]

The momentum of the movement evoked opposition from the Arya Samaj section, who apprehended that the Government might not enter into negotiations with the Sikhs again. A deputation comprising Virendra, a Congressite and Arya Samajist, Narain Dass and Harikishan Dass, General-Secretary and Vice-President of Sanatam Dharam Pratinidhi Sabha respectively, Acharya Ram Dev, President of Arya Pratinidhi Sabha and Jagat Narain, then an M.L.A., waited on the Prime Minister on June 16, 1960 and assured him that the Hindus would give full co-operation in the maintenance of law and order, conveying thereby in the suppression of the Sikhs, and that the Punjabi Suba demand was actually a step to the Sikh independent State, and must be resisted.[79]

The Prime Minister speaking on the Independence Day, August 15, 1960 at Delhi called the movement, "a stage tamasha going on in Delhi and Punjab about the Punjabi Suba," and declared, "that this demand might be good or bad, but there were many wrong things in the movement, and there is danger to the freedom of the country. The Punjabi language is a great language, a virile language and I want that every Punjabi should himself consider learning both Hindi and Punjabi, but there could be no bifurcation of Punjab." Chief Minister Kairon also speaking on the same occasion at Chandigarh declared that Punjab would maintain its bilingual character.[80]

After failure to convince the government by constitutional and agitational means, Sant Fateh Singh, the Vice President of the Akali Dal, pledged to achieve his mission through sacrifice so as to rouse the conscience of the authorities. While highlighting his aim, he said, "You have closed all the doors for justice and fair play. I am left with no way out but to go to fast-unto-death as to pick your conscience".[81] On December 18, he took an oath at the Akal Takhat and started his fast-unto-death. In a number of appeals, Nehru asked Sant Fateh Singh to give up his fast, promised to do everything possible for the advancement of Punjabi language, but left no doubt about his opposition to the demand for Punjabi Suba which he thought would be harmful for the Sikhs, Punjab and India.[82] Subsequently, on January 4, 1961 in a move to bring about the end of the fast, the Government released Master Tara Singh.

Master Tara Singh on his release was given a tremendous welcome, and the Working Committee of the Akali Dal in its meeting on January 5, 1961, passed the following resolution :[83]

> The Working Committee of the Shiromani Akali Dal has discussed the entire situation created by the Punjabi Suba movement and Sant Fateh Singh's fast in its two-day meeting under the Presidentship of Master Tara Singh. The statement of the Prime Minister dated 31 December, 1960, that he had sent his request to Sant Fateh Singh to come and convince him of the justness of the demand of Punjabi Suba before resorting to fast and also the telegram of the Prime Minister to Sant Fateh Singh from Bhavnagar, has also been dispassionately considered by the Working Committee. The Working Committee is of the view that though more effective methods to communicate the Prime Minister's request for opening talks on the question of Punjabi Suba should have been adopted to avoid later unhappy development, yet it is of the view, that the offer of negotiations and talks on the question of the unilingual Punjabi State made by the Prime Minister, should be

considered in the hope that an honest effort will be made by the Government of India to understand and concede the demand made by the Shiromani Akali Dal on its merits.

On 9 January, Sant Feteh Singh broke his fast on the urging of Master Tara Singh. After breaking his fast, Sant held three round of talks with Nehru, but the talks between Nehru and Sant ended in failure.[84] After failure of talks, Master Tara Singh now decided to undertake a fast-unto-death himself in order to coerce the government into conceding Punjabi Suba. On August 15, 1961, Indian's Independence day, Master Tara Singh started his fast-unto-death after taking an oath in the Golden Temple that he would not break his fast until Nehru accepted the demand for Punjabi Suba.[85]

Meanwhile, in Golden Temple, Akali leaders delivered strong speeches threatening the government with violence in case Master Tara Singh died.[86] Chief Minister Kairon had, however, been able to maintain complete law and order in the state. He had pledged that he would not let a single leaf stir in the Punjab and he lived up to the reputation he had built himself as the "iron man" of Punjab. When the Communists decided to participate in the agitation in the belief that they would follow the death of the Akali leader, Kairon arrested their chief leaders before they had a chance to go underground. Kairon further established the principle that the Gurdwaras could no longer remain "privileged sanctuaries" if they gave refuge to people for whom the police had issued warrants. Kairon's personal network of intelligence sources kept him informed of the various activities within the Akali headquarters.[87]

The Punjab Government and the Congress leaders embarked on the old strategy of inspiring statements by Hindu leaders, and handy Sikhs, in condemning the demand for Punjabi Suba and the fast of Master Tara Singh. The Hindu Raksha Sammelan, representing various organisations of the Hindus, passed a resolution on June 12, 1961, that "the Hindi Raksha Samiti is most anxious that an early and satisfactory solution of the language controversy should be found out. It is, however, most essential that the solution of this problem should be based on a recognition of the fact that Punjab is a bilingual state, where both languages, Hindi and Punjabi have to flourish side by side without any restriction or compulsion".[88]

The firm policy at the Central Government in regard to the Enquiry Commission and Kairon's effective maintenance of law and order convinced the Akalis that they were fighting a losing battle.[89] Once again they called off their talks with the Government, but finally agreed to the appointment of an Enquiry Commission on the Government's terms and Master Tara Singh ended his 48 days fast on 1 October, 1961. The same day, the Government issued a statement about its decision to appoint a commission which 'may go into the general question of discrimination and examine any charges of alleged differential treatment or grievances of the Sikhs.[90]

The Enquiry Commission comprising S.K. Das, former Chief Justice of India, M.C. Chhagla and C.P. Ramaswamy Ayyer, was appointed to hear the grievances of the Sikhs of the Punjab.[91] But Master Tara Singh chose to boycott it on the plea that certain names suggested by him had not been accepted for the Commission by the Government.[92] The Akalis of all shades refused to cooperate with it.[93] The Commission submitted its report in February 1962. It reported that no discrimination against the Sikhs, could be established as they were over-represented in the public services and in the Punjab cabinet.[94] The appointment and finding of the Commission failed to satisfy the aspiration of the Akali Dal. The Akali morcha had failed to achieve its objectives. The failure of the Akali agitation had a deep impact on Akali politics.[95]

In the meantime, Punjab was in the midst of the third general elections of the country in January and February 1962.[96] Master Tara Singh asked for a referendum on the Punjabi Suba issue in the so-called Punjabi-speaking region. Congress leaders proposed that the forthcoming general elections in 1962 be considered a referendum. At first, Master Tara Singh refused but later on, when coercing the government failed, he accepted the challenge to fight the elections on the issue of Punjabi Suba. The elections soon became for the Akali Dal a 'war' for Punjabi Suba, with their immediate aim as the defeat of the Congress party by mobilising all anti-government forces.[97]

The Akali Dal now started negotiations with the other political parties in the Punjab to break through its own isolation and to confront the Congress party, especially its "big guns" with a joint opposition. The wide ideological differences among these parties precluded an overall electoral alliance, but the Akali Dal was able to arrange in about 40 constituencies and managed to make electoral adjustments of some sort with these parties ranging from the extreme right (the Swantantra Party) to the extreme left (the Communist Party) with the Republican Party and the Praja Socialist Party in between.[98]

Some of these electoral adjustments, however, had their limitations. If the Communist Party and the Republican Party associated too closely with the Akali Dal, they could lose Hindu and Harijan votes, yet they could not get Sikh votes without doing precisely that. Furthermore, these arrangements provided the Congress party with an effective propaganda point that the opposition parties had nothing in common ideologically and that the strange alliances and "political marriages" were merely to defeat the Congress.[99] The Akali Dal did not reach any agreement with the Jan Sangh on electoral adjustments, but the Congress leaders and other observers alleged the existence of a secret alliance between the two parties.[100]

The approach of the Congress leadership in the selection of its candidates was to select those that could be depended upon to play an anti-Suba role and it is for this reason that many of the erstwhile Akalis, who had joined the Congress in 1956 as a result of merger of the Akali Dal in the Congress and had not toed anti-Sikh line, were deliberately not selected as candidates. The entire government machinery was set to motion in support of the Congress candidates. The Congress party, no doubt, was able to capture 90 seats out of 154 in the

Punjab and Chief Minister Kairon was declared successful.[101]

The Akali Dal contested as an independent party, but could not win more than 19 out of 154 seats. The Akali Dal was unable to win a majority even in the Punjabi-speaking region of the Punjab.[102] Of the 89 seats in the so-called Punjabi-speaking region, the Akali Dal was able to win only 19 seats and secured only 19.8 percent of the total votes polled. In Punjab as a whole, the Akali Dal obtained only 11.7 percent of the votes, with no seats outside the Punjabi-speaking region. The two other parties on record as supporting Punjabi Suba, at least as conceived, were the Communist Party and the Praja Socialist Party, which received 10 percent and 0.7 percent respectively of the total votes polled in the Punjabi-speaking region. The Jan Sangh, which vigorously opposed the demand of Punjabi Suba, secured 7.7 percent of the vote in the same region while the Congress party polled 45.8 per cent of the vote.[103]

Table 4.4. 1962 Election Results by Regions in Punjab[104]

Political Group	*Punjabi-speaking region*			*Hindi-speaking region*		
	Number	*% Age*	*Seats*	*Number*	*% Age*	*Seats*
Congress	1,807,427	45.8	51	1,136,412	40.9	39
Akali Dal	780,105	19.8	19	9,820	0.4	—
Communist Party	396,080	10.0	9	97.830	3.5	—
Jan Sangh	302,130	7.7	4	337,435	12.1	4
Republican Party (SCF)	111,441	2.8	—	33,599	1.2	—
Swatantra Party	93,484	2.4	—	167,792	6.0	3
Praja Socialist	28,231	0.7	—	32,159	1.1	—
Independents	425,556	10.8	6	869,340	31.3	19
Others	1,835	—	—	96,293	3.5	—
Total	**3,946,28**	**100.0**	**89**	**2,780,680**	**100.0**	**65**

The general elections of 1962 did little to clear the atmosphere. The Congress party won in most mixed constituencies; Akali supporters of the Punjabi Suba carried the majority of Sikh voters. Before the Akalis could mature their plans to make another bid for the Suba, however, the Chinese invaded the Indian frontiers. The Sikhs suspended their agitation and eagerly joined in the defence of the country.[105] All the Sikhs responded well. Punjab contributed more than 20 million rupees to the national defence fund, besides gold weighing double the weight of Jawaharlal Nehru.[106]

Meanwhile, Kairon's leadership came to be openly criticised by a number of legislators. They submitted a charge sheet against him to the Congress President. A deputation of some opposition leaders had already met the President of India with over thirty charges of corruption, nepotism and favouritism against Kairon. Such charges in fact had been brought against him in 1958, but he was then strongly supported by Jawaharlal Nehru to ensure that the Punjab Legislators did not pass a vote of no confidence against him. Even in 1963, Jawaharlal Nehru was inclined to support him, but opposition was now stronger and more vocal.[107]

On October 22, 1963, Nehru recommended to the President that an enquiry might be made into the charges against Kairon. He added, however, that any change in the leadership of the Punjab might result in producing confusion and putting a stop to the progress that the state was making under him.[108] In 1963, the President of India at Nehru's behalf appointed a one man Commission named by Justice S.R. Dass to enquire into the various charges levelled against Kairon.[109] The enquiry Commission started its work on 5 September, 1963.

Nehru's refusal to suspend Kairon led to the resignation of a few Congress legislators. Kairon believed that Prime Minister Nehru would come to his rescue, but unfortunately for him Nehru passed away in May 1964.[110] The Commission's findings were against Kairon. He resigned on 14 June, 1964, a week before the publication of the Commission's verdict. In the meantime, Kairon was assassinated in February 1965.[111] After Kairon's death, the Congress was left without any powerful leader who could resist the demand for a Punjabi-speaking state.

In August, 1965, Sant Feteh Singh announced that he would go on a fast-unto-death from 10 September, 1965 and will immolate himself if he survived the fast for 15 days. In the meantime, the war between India and Pakistan broke out on 5 September, 1965.[112] The Sant announced on 9 September, 1965, a day before his fast was to begin that he would put off his intended fast to some later day after the end of the war.[113] All sections of the Punjabis once again displayed great patriotic fervour during the three weeks of war till the cease-fire was declared on 26 September, 1965.[114]

Soon after the announcement of cease-fire, the Union Home Minister made a statement that the question of the Punjabi-province would be examined all afresh and Parliamentary Committee under the Chairmanship of Hukam Singh, the Speaker, would be set up. A cabinet sub-committee was formed to advise the Parliamentary Committee from time to time. It consisted of Indira Gandhi, Y.B. Chavan and Mahavir Tyagi.[115]

The situation on the issue was still fluid when news came of the death of Lal Bahadur Shastri at Tashkent on January 11, 1966. Mrs. Indira Gandhi was elected leader of the party and Prime Minister on January 20, 1966.[116] On 9 March, 1966, the Congress Working Committee recommended to the Union Government that a state with Punjabi as state language might be created out of the existing Punjab. The Home Minister, Gulzari Lal Nanda, announced the appointment of a Commission on 17 April, 1966.[117]

The Parliamentary Committee decided in favour of reorganisation of Punjab on linguistic basis. Immediately after the decision to reorganise Punjab had been announced, the state Jan Sangh expressed its grim determination to oppose and resist it by all constitutional and peaceful means. It even appointed a five-men action committee to carry on an agitation to force its reversal. However, within weeks of formation of the Suba, the Jan Sangh leadership moved to accommodating status. It not only accepted it, but also advised Hindus to own Punjabi.[118] Touring Punjab in April 1966, M.S. Golwalker, the RSS Sarasangchalak called upon Punjabi Hindus to learn Punjabi and to accept it as their mother tongue.[119]

The Punjab Reorganisation Bill, providing for the creation of Haryana and Punjab, was introduced in the Lok Sabha on 3 September, 1966 and passed on 7 September. It received the President's assent on 18 September. The Punjabi-speaking state was inaugurated on 1 November, 1966.

REFERENCES

1. B.R. Nayar : *Minority Politics in the Punjab,* Princeton University Press, Princeton (1966), p. 26.
2. *Ibid.,* pp. 26-27.
3. *The Tribune,* (Ambala) 14 January, 1953.
4. B.R. Nayar : *Op. cit.,* p. 28.
5. *Ibid.,* pp. 76-77.
6. *Ibid.*
7. K.C. Gulati : *The Akali : Past and Present,* Ashajanak Publications, New Delhi (1974), p. 72.
8. B.R. Nayar : *Op. cit.,* p. 79.
9. *Ibid.*
10. Khushwant Singh : *A History of the Sikhs, (1839-1974)* Vol. II, Oxford University Press, Delhi (1966), p. 237.
11. *Ibid.,* p. 242.
12. *Ibid.,* pp. 250-51.
13. Satya M. Rai : *Punjab Since Partition,* Durga Publications, Delhi (1986), p. 60.
14. *The Tribune,* 25 February, 1946.
15. Maulana Abul Kalam Azad : *India wins Freedom,* Bombay (1959), pp. 128-30.
16. Satya M. Rai : *Op. cit.,* p. 61.
17. Khushwant Singh : *Op. cit.,* p. 257.

18. B.R. Nayar : *Op. cit.*, p. 93.
19. Campbell Johnson : *A Mission with Mountbatten,* Robert Hal, London (1951), p. 191.
20. Khushwant Singh : *Op. cit.*, p. 287.
21. Feroz Chand : *"What is happening in East Punjab?"* N.C. (It is not certain what 'N.C.' stands for perhaps Indian News Chronicle) April 8, 1948.
22. Harbans Singh : *The Statesman,* April 4, 1948.
23. Feroz Chand : *Op. cit.*, April 8, 1948.
24. Political Observer, *The Tribune,* April 10, 1949.
25. Satya M. Rai : *Op. cit.*, p. 269.
26. *Papers Relating to Hindi Agitation in Punjab* (Chandigarh, Public Relations Department, 1957), p. II.
27. *Akali Patrika,* 22 October, 1922.
28. *Ibid.*, 23 January, 1951.
29. Anup Chand Kaur : *The Punjab Crisis,* S. Chand & Co. Ltd., New Delhi (1985), p. 154.
30. *National Herald* (editorial) 6 November, 1949.
31. *The Tribune,* (editorial) 16 May, 1951.
32. *Ibid.*, 6 April, 1951.
33. *Loc. cit.*
34. B.R. Nayr : *Op. cit.*, p. 217.
35. Krishan Gopal : *Dynamics of Punjabi Suba Movement,* Deep and Deep Publications Ltd., New Delhi (1999), pp. 105-6.
36. K.C. Gulati : *Op. cit.*, p. 161.
37. *Ibid.*
38. A.S. Narang : *Punjab Politics in National Perspective,* Geetanjali Publishing House, New Delhi (1986), p. 33.
39. K.C. Gulati : *Op. cit.*, p. 162.
40. *Why Maha Punjab,* Memorandum by Punjab Jan Sangh, Joshi Printing Press, Ambala Cantt, n.d., p. 2.
41. Satya M. Rai : *Op. cit.*, pp. 281-83.
42. Surinder Singh Parmar : *History of Bhartiya Jan Sangh in*

Punjab, (unpublished Ph.D. Thesis) Punjab University, Chandigarh (1987), p. 183.

43. *The Indian Express,* 19 April, 1955.
44. *Resolutions of State Reorganisation,* 1920-56, All Indian Congress Committee, New Delhi, n.d.
45. Gulshan Rai : *Formation of Haryana,* B.R. Publishing Corporation, Delhi (1987), p. 69.
46. *Hindustan Times,* 17 October, 1955.
47. Papers relating to Hindi Agitation in Punjab : *Op. cit.,* p. 9.
48. Satya M. Rai : *Op. cit.,* p. 297.
49. *The Tribune,* 16 March, 1956.
50. *Ibid.,* 26 June, 1956.
51. *The Spokesman,* III, No : 12, March 25, 1953.
52. *The Tribune,* May 25, 1956.
53. *Loc. cit.*
54. *The Times of India,* 9 June, 1956 and *The Tribune,* 12 June, 1956.
55. *The Tribune,* 16 July, 1956.
56. B.R. Nayar : *Op. Cit.,* p. 226.
57. *The Spokesman,* VI, No : 40 October 8, 1956.
58. B.R. Naryar : *Op. cit.,* p. 227.
59. K.C. Gulati : *Op. cit.,* p. 165.
60. B.R. Nayar : *Op. cit.,* p. 228.
61. K.C. Gulati : *Op. cit.,* p. 166.
62. Krishan Gopal : *Op. cit.,* p. 239.
63. Myren Weiner and John Osgood Field : *Electoral Politics in the Indian States : Party Systems and Cleavages,* Manohar Book Service, Delhi (1975), p. 39.
64. Complied from Election Commission, *Report on the Second General Elections in India, 1957,* Vol. II, Manager Publications, Delhi (1958).
65. A.S. Narang : *Op. cit.,* p. 37.
66. B.R. Nayar : *'Punjab'* in Myron Weiner (ed.) : *State Politics in India,* Princeton University Press, Princeton (1968), pp. 458-80.

67. J.S. Garewal : *The New Cambridge History of India : The Sikhs of The Punjab,* Orient Longman, Cambridge University, Cambridge (1990), p. 196.
68. A.S. Sarhadi : *Punjabi Suba : The Story of Struggle,* U.G. Kapoor and Sons, Delhi (1974), p. 309.
69. Jaswant Singh (ed.) : *Master Tara Singh : Jiwan Sangarsh Te Udesh,* Hardes Printing Press, Amritsar (1972), pp. 287-88.
70. A.S. Sarhadi : *Op. cit.,* pp. 312-14.
71. *Ibid.,* p. 315.
72. B.R. Nayar : *Op. cit.,* pp. 247-48.
73. Harbans Singh : *The Heritage of the Sikhs,* Manohar Publisher, Delhi (1983), p. 328.
74. *Punjabi Sube Te Morche Da Itihas* by Sikh Scholars, Amritsar, Gurbani Parkashan (1960), p. 15.
75. Harinder Singh Dilgeer : *Shiromani Akali Dal,* Punjabi Book Company, Jullundhar (1970), p. 242.
76. Sant Fateh Singh : *Facts about Punjabi Suba Agitation,* Amritsar, (1960), p. 4.
77. *Punjabi Sube Te Morche Da Itihas,* p. 18.
78. B.R. Nayar : *Op. cit.,* p. 249.
79. A.S. Sarhadi : *Op. cit.,* p. 331.
80. *Ibid.*
81. Sant Fateh Singh : *Abhul Yaadan,* Ganganagar (1962), p. 19.
82. B.R. Nayar : *Op. cit.,* p. 252.
83. *The Tribune,* 26 January, 1961.
84. Shiromani Akali Dal : *Synopsis of the Nehru-Fateh Singh Talks on the issue of the formation of the Punjabi-speaking State,* Secretary, Shiromani Akali Dal, Amritser (1961).
85. B.R. Nayar : *Op. cit.,* p. 255.
86. Punjab Public Relation Department, sidelines on *Akali Strategy,* Chandigarh : Controller, Printing and Stationary (1961), pp. 3-24.
87. B.R. Nayar : *Op. cit.,* p. 258.
88. A.S. Sarhadi : *Op. cit.,* p. 353.
89. *The Tribune,* 18 September, 1961.

90. *The Spokesman*, XI-A, No : 8, October, 9 (1961).
91. *The Hindu*, 1 November, 1961.
92. Gurmit Singh : *History of the Sikh Struggle*, Atlantic Publishers, New Delhi (1989), p. 146.
93. V.R. Adiraju : *Sikhs and India : Identity Crisis*, Satya Publications, Hyderabad (1991), pp. 143-44.
94. Kamlesh Kumar Wadhwa : *Minority Safeguards in India*, Thomson Press (India) Ltd., Faridabad (1975), p. 166.
95. S.C. Arora : *Turmoil in Punjab Politics*, Mittal Publications, New Delhi (1990), p. 71.
96. A.S. Sarhadi : *Op. cit.*, p. 376.
97. *"Honewala Chunao Ghamsaan"* (The Impending Election Battle), *Prabhat*, 13 November, 1961.
98. B.R. Nayar : *Op. cit.*, p. 206.
99. *Ibid.*, pp. 206-07.
100. *The Tribune*, February 20, 1962.
101. A.S. Sarhadi : *Op. cit.*, p. 376.
102. J.C. Anand : *"Punjab Politics of Retreating Communalism"* in Iqbal Narain (ed.) : *State Politics in India*, Meenakshi Prakashan, Meerut (1976), p. 264.
103. B.R. Nayar : *Op. cit.*, p. 210.
104. Compiled from Election Commission, *Report on the Third General Election in India, 1962*, Part II, Manager Publications, Delhi (1963).
105. Khushwant Singh : *Op. cit.*, p. 301.
106. J.S. Garewal : *The Akalis : A Short History*, Punjab Studies Publication, Chandigarh, p. 134.
107. *Ibid.*
108. *Ibid.*
109. S.C. Arora : *Op. cit.*, p. 62.
110. Karishan Gopal : *Op. cit.*, p. 264.
111. J.S. Garewal : *Op. cit.*, p. 135.
112. *Indian Express*, 16 August, 1965.
113. *The Tribune*, 10 September, 1965.

114. Krishan Gopal : *Op. cit.*, p. 269.
115. J.S. Garewal : *Op. cit.*, p. 136.
116. A.S. Sarhadi : *Op. cit.*, p. 421.
117. J.S. Garewal : *Op. cit.*, p. 137.
118. *The Hindustan Times*, 21 March, 1966.
119. *Ibid.*, 4 April, 1966.

5

Congress and Formation of Punjabi Suba

The Indian National Congress is a secular, broad based, all India political party. The party's ideology is firmly committed to parliamentary democracy and planned economic development for the welfare of Indian people. It is a coalition of diverse political and social groups and, in its historical growth, has developed the machinery and skills to aggregate a variety of groups and viewpoints. The party rejects identification with any particular religion or caste; its membership is open to all, regardless of their religion, caste or linguistic affiliation.[1]

Before independence, the Congress party had become the strongest political force, the embodiment of nationalism unlike other political parties, which were regional, sectional or sectarian in character. As a result, it succeeded to the government after the end of British rule in India. Since independence, the Congress party has remained in unchallenged control of the government at the centre for a number of decades because the opposing parties represented the local or regional pockets of strength, whereas the strength and organisation of the Congress party were spread all over India. The control of the Congress party at the Centre enabled it further, formally or informally to assist its state branches to remain in power in the states, which in turn helped it to maintain the party in power at the centre.[2]

At midnight on 15 August, 1947, the Constitutent Assembly declared India to be independent. Its first Prime Minister, Jawaharlal Nehru gave an inspiring message (Tryst with Destiny) to its citizens. A long cherished vision had materialized, a new hope had come into being and the citizens of this great country were on the verge of a bold advance. Whatever their religion, castes or creed, they were considered equal citizen of India with equal rights, privileges and obligations. Nehru remembered at that moment (in his speech) the sorrow-stricken homeless thousands, who were coming to the country or leaving it. They had to be resettled and rehabilitated. The Indian Government retained the responsibility of rehabilitating urban refugees. The rural refugees in Punjab had to be resettled by the Punjab Government. Dr. Gopi Chand Bhargava was the first Chief Minister of Punjab, who enjoyed the support of Sardar Vallabh Bhai Patel at the centre.[3]

Punjab, immediately after the partition, was faced with a number of other problems and the Akali party extended its whole-hearted support to the Congress in all political matters.[4] In fact, Master Tara Singh gave a rebuff to the Pakistan propaganda that there was a demand for a Sikh state in the following words : "The bogey of the Sikh state in the East Punjab, is being conjured up by the Pakistan propaganda machine in order to create dissensions between the Hindus and the Sikhs. The Hindus and the Sikhs will rise and fall together. Their fates are inextricably linked".[5]

However, the demand for a Punjabi-speaking state was made in February 1948. Master Tara Singh, the Akali leader, criticised the Government of India's policy of not referring the question of demarcation of boundaries of Punjab to a Commission. Changing drastically his earlier stance, he said, "We have a culture different from the Hindus. Our culture is Gurmukhi culture and our literature is also in the Gurmukhi script." He added, "We want to have a province where we can safeguard our culture and our tradition."[6]

'The Tribune' in its leaderette of the 12 November, 1949, wrote, "Why the Sikhs should show such a dread of the so-called Hindu majority in Punjab, when they are ready to accept the Hindu majority at the Centre which has a far greater power than the provinces, we don't know? The logic of the communal fanatic defies rational understanding. He is so desperately keen on promoting his own claims and he forgets that other interests and claims are to be reckoned with."[7]

Discussing further the implication of the demand, it said, "Again, why should a Hindu minority in a proposed Sikh province remain under a permanent Sikh majority if the Sikhs show such a distrust of the Hindu majority. The logic of the communalist leads straight the exchange of the population and to the establishment of an independent state".[8] Such writings also appeared in the Arya Samaj press in the East Punjab.

The Congress leadership did not concede the demand. It was in such a bitter atmosphere that Hukam Singh, the then Akali representative in the Lok Sabha, explaining the stand of the Akali Dal at a press conference at Bombay on 1 January, 1950, said, "The demand for the reconstitution of Punjab on a linguistic basis, through an impartial agency sponsored by the Shiromani Akali Dal, is the only means for the preservation of the Punjabi culture and language. It is a perfectly democratic demand and only a most perverse imagination can label it as communal. We, infact, expect the Congress to fulfill all its pledges to the minorities."[9]

The writings in the Punjab Hindu Press concerning the demand of Punjabi Suba by the Shiromani Akali Dal became so vile and vulgar, and took such an abusive turn that this evoked a very illuminating and informative article from the pen of Arthur Moore,[10] a well meaning Englishman. Arthur Moore wrote in the weekly 'Thought' on October 29, 1949 : "We must learn by our mistakes. It is bad enough that we have today two nations in the Indian sub-continent. Let us not do anything that might lead to the creation of the third."[11]

The Congress policy to spearhead the opposition to the creation of the Punjabi linguistic state created a rift between the Congress and the Sikhs after nearly 2½ years of collaboration and cooperation and began to wear the Sikhs away from the Congress. It was then that the Shiromani *Akali Dal* issued a show cause notice in early July 1950 to the *Panthic*

MLA's, who had merged in the Congress assembly party in early 1948, why they should not leave Congress party and have a block of their own.[12]

This move of the *Shiromani Akali Dal* sparked off a strong opposition of the Congress amongst the Sikhs, which made the Congress High Command mobilise its forces amongst the Sikhs to oppose the creation of a linguistic state. It was then that Partap Singh Kairon, the then President of Punjab State Congress announced his extreme opposition to the division of the state on a linguistic basis. He also said that the need of the hour was to extend the boundaries of Punjab and he also declared that he would spearhead the movement amongst the Sikhs in order to oppose the creation of a linguistic state. It was then and thereafter that the Congress openly started opposing a linguistic state in Punjab.[13]

On 20 January, 1951, Gopi Chand Bhargava resigned as a Chief Minister and the Punjab was placed under President's rule due to factions in the Punjab Congress.[14] However, the first general elections were held in 1952. The Congress and the Akali Dal were the main contenders for power. The elections in 1952 were fought on the basis of Punjabi Suba. Pandit Nehru in his electioneering tour strongly opposed the creation of a Punjabi Suba. Speaking at Patiala on 4 January, 1952, when a few All India Sikh Students Federation activists like Amarjeet Singh Ahluwalia, Gursewak Singh and Tarlochan Singh in the meeting interrupted him during his speech by shouting out the slogans, "Le Ke Rahenge Punjabi Suba." Nehru declared, "I will not allow India to be divided again. I will not allow any further trouble. If there is any trouble in any part of India, I would put it down with all my strength."[15]

By the time of First General Elections, both the Akali Dal and the Hindu organisations such as the Jan Sangh and the Arya Samaj had become distrustful of each other and appealed to the religious and linguistic sentiments of voters.[16] In these state assembly elections, Congress won 96 seats (76.1%) out of 126 total seats. Table 5.1 shows that out of these 96 elected candidates 36 were Sikhs, 57 were Hindus and 3 were Muslims.

The Akali Dal was able to win (10.3%) seats and all its candidates were Sikhs. CPI got 5 (3.9%) seats and all its nominees were Sikhs. Jan Sangh captured only 2 (1.5%) seats, one was a Hindu and the other was a Sikh. One Hindu candidate of Praja Socialist party won and 9 (7.1%) independents, out of which 5 were Hindus and 4 were Sikhs.[17] The Congress formed the ministry under the Chief Ministership of Bhim Sen Sachar in May 1952.

Table 5.1. 1952 Punjab Assembly Elections

Name of the Party	*Hindus*	*Sikhs*	*Muslims*	*Total*	*% of seats*
Congress	57	36	3	96	76.1%
Akali Dal	—	13	—	13	10.3%
CPI	—	5	—	5	3.9%
Jan Sangh	1	1	—	2	1.5%
Praja Socialist Party	1	—	—	1	0.7%
Independents	5	4	—	9	7.1%
Total	**64(51%)**	**59(47.1%)**	**3(2.3%)**	**126**	**100%**

Source : Punjab Election Office, Chandigarh.

In the meantime, the Government of India announced the formation of States Reorganisation Commission in 1953. Its formation by itself was a sign of hope for the Akalis, but Jawaharlal Nehru repeated his declaration against a Punjabi-speaking state during the Pepsu mid-term polls in early 1954.[18] In the 1954 mid-term polls in Pepsu, the Congress party won 22 seats with 40.4 percent votes as against the Akali Dal victory on 10 seats with 27.6 percent votes.[19] The ministry was formed by the Congress, headed by Col. Raghubir Singh, but the power was mainly in the hands of Brish Bhan.[20]

The State Reorganisation Commission had three members with Syed Fazil Ali as Chairman and H.N. Kunjru and K.M. Pannikar as members. The Akali Dal submitted memorandum urging the formation of a Punjabi-speaking state. The Akali Dal urged the formation of Punjabi Suba by merging the Punjabi-speaking areas of Punjab, Pepsu and Rajasthan on the basis of language.[21]

The Punjab Government advocated the formation of the Maha Punjab, which was more or less on the same lines as suggested by the Hindu Congressmen.[22] Several Hindu bodies opposed the demand by asking for the amalgamation of Himachal Pradesh and the Punjab into Maha Punjab.[23]

The States Reorganisation Commission did not accept the Akali Dal's demand for a Punjabi-speaking state, as there did not exist among the people of Punjab a "minimum measure of agreement necessary for making a change in the present set-up."[24]

The efforts to achieve their end were stepped up by all the political parties. With a view to check the popular upsurge and maintain peaceful conditions, the Punjab government imposed ban on shouting of slogans including that of the "Punjabi Suba". The Akalis threatened direct action—'morcha,' but the Government of India declared that it was prepared to meet the challenge.[25] On May 10, Master Tara Singh led out the first batch of 10 volunteers in defiance of the ban. He was denied along with his companion.[26] The climax was reached on 4 July, when the police raided certain buildings attached to the Golden Temple in a bid to flush out the so-called aiders and abettors of the movement from their sanctuaries.'[27]

On July 12, the ban was formally withdrawn. The Chief Minister, Bhim Sen Sachar, presented himself at the Akal Takhat and in an open 'divan' apologised on behalf of the government for the sacrilege committed by the police on July 4.[28] The apology cost him his office. Partap Singh Kairon, who commanded a majority in the Congress party, sent a sufficient large numbers of his supporters to meet the Prime Minister and tell him, how, Sachar had mishandled the agitation. The charge against the Chief Minister was that instead of taming the Akalis, he had pampered them. Sachar offered his resignation to Nehru and it was accepted.[29]

After Sachar's resignation, Sardar Partap Singh Kairon was unanimously elected as its leader by the Congress Legislature Party on January 21, 1956. Mr. Kairon started with a three members cabinet, which were Pt. Mahan Lal, Prof. Sher Singh and S. Gurbachan Singh Bajwa. The ministry was expanded about four months later. The ministry continued up to 31 October, 1956, when Pepsu area was merged with the erstwhile East Punjab to form the state of Punjab. On 1 November, 1956 after his re-election as the leader of the new Congress Legislature Party, Mr. Kairon reconstituted the ministry and added five more ministers and five deputy ministers. This was done primarily to give due representation in the cabinet to the erstwhile Pepsu area.[30]

Thus in October, 1956, a convention of Akali Dal was held at Amritsar in which were present, the members of its Working Committee, the Akali MLA's from Punjab and Pepsu, the representatives of the District Akali Jathas and other prominent leaders from different parts of the country. The convention formally decided by a resolution to amend the constitution of the Akali Dal, so as to confine its activities to religious, educational, cultural, social and economic betterment of the Sikhs. It was further resolved that in regard to the political activities, the members of the Dal should join the Congress.[31]

It was in accordance with this decision that the Akalis fought the 1957 elections on Congress ticket. The Congress accommodated 26 former Akalis. But this did not satisfy Master Tara Singh, who in spite of the merger had himself not joined the Congress party in his personal capacity and wanted a quota of approximately 40 seats. Dissatisfied (despite the formal agreement) Master Tara Singh set up more than 15 candidates of his own, whom he called "Panthic candidates". He also strongly spoke against the Congress party declaring that it was futile to repose confidence any more in the Congress party as "the Congress had deceived us."[32]

In the 1957 general elections, the Congress polled more votes in the assembly as well as parliamentary elections than it had done in 1952. In Punjab, the Congress won 120 seats, including 28 contested by ex-Akalis and polled 47.5 percent of the votes. The number of Congress votes in the Punjabi-speaking or Sikh majority area was still higher, 48.5 percent, see table 5.2.[33] The Akalis polled about 20 percent of the votes in Punjabi-speaking region, though without winning a single seat. The Congress formed a stable government under the leadership of Partap Singh Kairon. The 1957 elections opened the Kairon era of carrot and stick. The carrot was meant for the less recalcitrant of the Chief Minister's adversaries and the stick for the more so.[34]

Table 5.2. Party Position in Punjab, 1957 Elections

Party	*Seats in Punjab*	*% of votes in Punjab*	*Seats in Punjabi Region*	*% of voters in Punjabi Region*
Congress	120	47.5	71	48.6
Jan Sangh	9	8.6	5	7.2
CPI	6	13.6	3	17.7
Other's & Independents	29	30.3	7	26.5

Source : Compiled from India Election Commission. *Report on the Second General Elections in India, 1957,* Vol. II, Delhi, Manager Publications, (1958), pp. 891-915.

In June 1958, Master Tara Singh announced that the Congress was not serious about the Regional Formula and, if nothing was done about it, the Akali Dal felt obliged to repudiate it. On 16th September, he announced that, since the Regional Formula had not been implemented in a satisfactory manner, he was compelled to reopen the issue of the Punjabi Suba. A Punjabi Suba conference was held at Amritsar on 12 October. The plan of action was announced by Sant Fateh Singh, the Senior Vice-President of Shiromani Akali Dal.[35]

In the meantime, Partap Singh Kairon planned to oust Master Tara Singh from the Shiromani Gurdwara Prabandhak Committee with the help of Giani Kartar Singh and Gian Singh Rarewala, both of whom were members of his cabinet. Early in 1959, Master Tara Singh lost the Presidential election of the SGPC by three votes. His defeat was interpreted as a defeat of his Punjabi-speaking state.[36]

At the Punjabi Suba conference held in Chandigarh, Master

Tara Singh disclosed his intentions of launching a mass movement on a vast scale. In preparation, a silent procession was to be taken out in Delhi on March 5, 1959. The government acted swiftly and took him into custody. The Delhi march did take place, with Sikhs participating from all over the country. The procession ended in a religious 'divan' at Gurdwara Rakab Ganz. Within a week, Master Tara Singh was released from Jail.[37]

The stage was now set for a renewal agitation. Master Tara Singh declared that he would contest the SGPC elections of 1960 on Punjabi Suba issue. In December 1959, the Congress High Command decided to bifurcate Bombay to create the States of Maharashtra and Gujarat. This left Punjab as the only bilingual state in the country.[38] Fortunately for the Akali Dal, Kairon once again made a mistake of challenging it to a trial of strength in its own fortress. Instead of the Khalsa Dal, which fought and lost the 1955 elections to the SGPC, the Congress nominees in the 1960 elections were fielded under the banner of Sadh Sangat Board.[39]

The election results (1960) were declared on the 19 January, 1960, when the Shiromani Akali Dal secured 132 seats out of 139. The Sadh Sangat Board secured 4 seats only, while the pro-Communist Desh Bhagat Board failed to get even one. Master Tara Singh was unanimously elected President of the SGPC at a general assembly meeting specially convinced for the purpose of March 7, 1960, where it was also decided to boycott the 26 member committee appointed by the state government to consider the language issue.[40] "The only solution of the linguistic trouble of Punjab," the resolution declared, "is to bifurcate Punjab on the basis of Punjabi and Hindi.[41]

To launch a morcha for the Punjabi Suba, it became necessary for the Akalis to first break away from the Congress. The Working Committee of the Shiromani Akali Dal directed the 'Akali' legislators to resign, but only five of them accepted this directive.[42] On 30 April, Master Tara Singh announced his intention to march to Delhi like a conquering hero with the avowed object of leading a procession to press for the formation of a Punjabi Suba. He was arrested on 21 May along with the five Akali legislators who had resigned from the Congress party.[43]

A reign of terror was created throughout the state. In spite of all this the Shiromani Akali Dal stuck to its programme of sending a 'Jatha' of 11 to Delhi without Master Tara Singh.[44] The Akali Dal was opening a war on two fronts. Its volunteers were going to court arrest both in Delhi and Amritsar simultaneously. The movement gained momentum as the time lapsed. Every day Jathas would come out of the precincts of the Darbar Sahib, peacefully and calmly, and court arrest. The routine courting of arrest at Amritsar was 21 daily, whereas it was 11 at Delhi, but more persons courted arrest when there was insistence by those gathered there. According to government's own admission 26,000 Sikhs were arrested.

On the absence of Master Tara Singh, Sant Fateh Singh, the then Senior Vice President of Shiromani Akali Dal took over as dictator of the 'morcha.' He was then a non-entity, but rose in power and stature in no time. Because of his advisers and appreciating techniques, the Sant began to clear the position regarding the nature of the Punjabi Suba demand.[45]

Accordingly, the Sant called a press conference and proclaimed that, "We do not seek a Sikh majority area; that we are not concerned with percentages; that we want the Punjabi Suba to comprise that area where Punjabi language is spoken; that it is immaterial whether the Sikhs are in majority or minority in such an area." He followed up this statement with a letter to Nehru worded in similar terms.[46]

On 29 October, 1960, Sant Fateh Singh wrote a letter to Prime Minister Jawaharlal Nehru drawing his attention to the large scale arrest of *Akalis* on faked charges, to the suppression of the entire Sikh press and to the reign of terror let loose by the government. In a firm reply, the Prime Minister made it clear to him that there could be no Punjabi Suba. On this Sant Fateh Singh announced his decision to go on to fast-unto-death on 18 December, 1960, for the achievement of Punjabi Suba.[47]

Sant Fateh Singh began his fast-unto-death on 18 December, 1960 in the presence of a huge gathering. In the course of a ten-minute speech, he directed the Sikhs to remain peaceful in the face of great provocation and said that his sacrifice would ultimately move the Government of India.[48] The Prime Minister Nehru, while addressing a public meeting at Delhi on 23 December made a personal appeal to Sant Fateh Singh to give up his fast and invited him for talks to Delhi.[49] Later, while speaking at the annual session of the Congress at Sardarnagar on 8 January, 1961, the Prime Minister Nehru said :

> It is not out of any discrimination against Punjab or distrust of the Sikhs that the process of forming a linguistic state was not possible after applying it elsewhere. I cannot accept the proposal that I should accept the principle of formation at a purely linguistic state. So far as Punjab is concerned, I am convinced that in the case of its division, it will be very harmful to Punjab, to the Sikhs as well as the Hindus, and to the whole of India. One of the leading and progressing states will fall back and get entangled in new problems.
>
> I have already stated in my Delhi speech on 31 December, 1960, what our views are about the Punjabi Suba and the Punjabi language. It is true that some persons of Punjab speak Hindi, but essentially Punjabi is the dominant language and should be encouraged in every way. Now I add one word to this because Master Tara Singh mentioned it to me about Sant Fateh Singh's having an oath and he should not be asked to break it. I do not like asking any person to break a solemn oath, but I am convinced that what I have said in my Delhi speech, and what I am stating today and the fact that I have placed before the country with regards to the Punjabi language, clearly meets the substance of what Sant Fateh Singh said. Oaths are not taken with regard to some legal aspect or statutory ways of looking at things, but about the substance of things. And therefore what I have stated should be

quite enough for Sant Fateh Singh to meet this difficulty and give up his fast.[50]

The speech pleased Master Tara Singh, whose immediate reaction was so favourable that he wired to the fasting Sant that, "I am satisfied with today's speech of the Prime Minister at Sardarnagar. Request to break your fast. It fulfills the requirements of vow."[51] The Akali Dal's Working Committee had a brief meeting near the venue of the fast and requested Sant Fateh Singh to give up his fast as the working Committee was satisfied with the statement of the Prime Minister.[52]

After breaking his fast Sant Fateh Singh met the Prime Minister at Delhi on 8 February, 1961. During these negotiations, Sant Fateh Singh emphasised the linguistic basis, which made Nehru more sympathitic than he had been before.[53] There were two more rounds, one on March 1, 1961 and the other on 12 May, 1961. But the talks between Nehru and Sant failed to produce any result.[54]

The negotiations with the government did not bear any fruit. Nehru refused to accept the contention that denial of a Punjabi-speaking province amounted to discrimination against the Sikhs. In sheer exasperation, Master Tara Singh undertook to fast-unto-death unless the Punjabi Suba was conceded. He began his fast on August 15, 1961 in the 'sanctuary' of the Golden Temple. The government refused to yield. After 43 days without food, the old warrior's spirit was broken and he gave up the self-imposed ordeal. Master Tara Singh saved his life but killed his political career and dealt a grievous blow to the cause of the Punjabi-speaking state.[55]

Prime Minister Nehru in a speech in the Parliament on 28 August and a statement to the press on 17 September said that a high level commission of enquiry would be set up to enquire into the charges of discrimination against the Sikhs.[56]

In pursuance of the above assurance, the Government of India set up a three man Commission, headed by S.R. Dass, to enquire into the various charges that had been made about discrimination against the Sikhs in Punjab. The other two members of the Commission were C.P. Ramaswamy Aiyer and M.C. Chagla.[57] A Government of India notification said, "The Commission will enquire into the general question of discrimination against the Sikhs and examine any charges of alleged differential treatment or grievances of the Sikhs."[58]

The Commission, which was appointed on 31 October, 1961, carried out its assignment despite its boycott by the Akali Dal.[59] It submitted its report to the Union Government on 19 February, 1962, in which it said, "On the materials before it, no case of discrimination against Sikhs in the Punjab has been made out."[60] The report said that, "Though they (Sikh) were only 34 percent of population of the Punjab, their representation in the Punjab Cabinet had always been 40 to 50 percent and they always had a Sikh in the Central Cabinet since 1947. There was a Sikh Governor of a State and several Sikh ambassadors and holders of important political positions."[61]

The Prime Minister, Nehru remained resolutely opposed to the creation of a Punjabi Suba until the end of his life. He too was convinced that the Akali demand was communal. He told the Parliament :[62]

> The whole of Punjab, whether it is in regard to language, whether it is in regard to ways of living, whether it is the food you eat and so many other things, it is unity whether it is Hindu or Sikh or I may add Muslim, now there are not many Muslims there. There are not those differences due to religion or due to language, which you find else where in India.

In the meantime, the Third General Elections (1962) of the country held in January and February 1962. The Akali Dal contested these elections primarily on Punjabi Suba issue. Once again the electorate rejected the demand for Punjabi Suba as out of 46 candidates fielded by Akali Dal in the Punjabi-speaking region, only 19 were successful and they obtained 11.7 percent of the total vote with no seats in the Hindu region.

On the other hand, Congress won 90 seats out of 154, and Kairon entered the second term of his Chief Ministership.[63] Kairon declared his determination that he would destroy

'Communalism', meaning thereby the entity of the Akali Party and their demand for the Punjabi Suba.[64] The internal situation in the country totally changed because of the border conflict with the Chinese forces, which had attacked country on October 22, 1962. They occupied a very large area. It was indeed painful to India to see how its defence collapsed before the invading army.[65]

Sant Fateh Singh temporarily suspended the Punjabi Suba movement in the wake of Indo-Chinese war and offered unconditional support to Nehru government in the war efforts.[66] The Working Committee of the Sant Akali Dal declared on December 23, 1962 that the demand for Punjabi Suba could not be pressed in view of the national emergency created by the Chinese invasion.[67]

Sant Fateh Singh met the Prime Minister on February 7, 1963 and presented a cheque of Rs. 50,000 on behalf of the Shiromani Gurdwara Parbandhak Committee as its contribution to the National Defence Fund.[68]

Speaking at a conference on February 16, 1963, Sant Fateh Singh said, "Our immediate objective is to drive out Chinese. The movement for the formation of Punjabi Suba has been slowed down, as it is a domestic problem. This demand will not be pressed during the emergency. We will again take up the issue after the Chinese are driven out."[69]

On the other hand, the iron-man of the Punjab, Partap Singh Kairon, who had checkmated the Punjabi Suba movement to a large extent had to face an enquiry on charges of corruption.[70] Earlier a deputation of the joint opposition Sant Akali Dal legislators had given a memorial to the President, Radha Krishnan, enumerating 32 charges of corruption, nepotism and favouritism against the Chief Minister. On 22 October, 1963, the Prime Minister had recommended to the President to have an inquiry made by some high authority into the charges levelled against the Chief Minister.[71]

S.R. Dass a retired Chief Justice of the Supreme Court was appointed as a one-man Commission to enquire into the charges. Nehru died on 27 May, 1964 before the Dass Commission was able to submit its report. By the time, the report was out, Lal Bahadur Shastri was Prime Minister, Kairon was left with no alternative but to resign from office. Ram Kishan succeeded him.[72]

The exit of Partap Singh Kairon from the political sphere of the state was a major event in Punjab politics, for he had ruled the state for 8 years, fighting all the while against the Akalis and their objectives. He was the one man who had not given way or surrendered despite the tremendous sacrifices, which the Sikhs had made for the attainment of Punjabi suba.[73]

With the changeover from Nehru to Shastri, matters came to head. The Sant had two meetings with Shastri on 7 and 8 August, 1965. Home Minister Nanda and Home Secretary L.P. Singh were present at these talks. The Sant made clear that his patience had been exhausted and unless the 'justice' done to the Sikhs by the Centre denying them Punjabi-speaking state was quickly righted they would be forced to resort to direct action.[74]

The Prime Minister Shastri told the Sant that it was in the larger interest of the country that Punjab should remain undivided and continue as a strong and prosperous state. He, however, assured him that he would do everything possible to remove the sense of grievances from the minds of the Sant and the Sikh community. A similar statement was made by Gulzari Lal Nanda, the then Home Minister of India, "While everything possible would be done to redress the genuine grievances of the Sikhs and to encourage Punjabi language, there was no question of dividing the strategic border state on linguistic, communal or any other basis."[75]

On 16 August, 1965, Sant declared before the Akal Takhat that he would begin his fast-unto-death on 10 September, 1965 and immolate himself on 25 September exactly at 9 a.m.[76] However, in view of the armed conflict with Pakistan, Sant Fateh Singh decided on 9 September to postpone his fast. It was much appreciated by the President of India, Dr. Sarvpalli Radhakrishnan.[77]

The cease-fire took place on September 26, 1965 on the intervention of the Security Council. The two great powers Soviet Union and U.S.A. interceded and used their good offices in this regard. Soon after the announcement of the cease-fire, the Government of India appointed a cabinet committee and a parliamentary sub-committee for the fresh examination of the Punjabi Suba issue.[78] The cabinet committee consisted of Indira Gandhi (the then Information and Broadcasting Minister) Y.B. Chawan (the then Defence Minister) and Mahavir Tyagi (the then Rehabilitation Minister), which would from time to time, advise the parliamentary committee to be set up with Hukam Singh, Speaker, as its President.[79]

On 2 March, 1966, the All India Congress Committee under the Presidentship of K.K. Kamraj passed a resolution favouring the reorganisation of Punjab on the basis of language. By this time, Indira Gandhi was in saddle as Prime Minister. Shastri died at Tashkent immediately after he had signed a peace pact with Pakistani President Ayub Khan.[80]

In the meantime, the Punjab Congress party took the initiative for the reorganisation of Punjab at the meeting of its Working Committee held on 9 March. It passed a resolution recommending to the Union Government to constitute a state with Punjabi as state language out of the existing Punjab.[81]

The decision of the Congress Working Committee was followed by large-scale disturbances in the main cities of Punjab. They were organised by the Jan Sangh and R.S.S. elements. They erupted simultaneously in all parts of Punjab on March 12, 1966. Buses, jeeps and other Government properties were set on fire in Amritsar, Jullundhar, Hissar, Panipat, and Ludhiana etc. At Ludhiana and some other places, it took a communal turn and there were clashes between Hindus and Sikhs. There were police firing in Amritsar.[82]

Shri Yagya Dutt Sharma, General Secretary of the Punjab and Himachal Jan Sangh, started a fast-unto-death at Amritsar on 9-3-1966 to protest against the proposed partition of Punjab. He went through this ordeal for 13 days and ended it on 21-3-1966. On that day, Shri A.B. Vajpayee issued a press statement to the effect that the Prime Minister and the Union Home Minister had given an assurance to preserve the unifying features of the overall unity of Punjab and also to provide all safeguards, linguistic and others, to the minorities, and further that the demarcation of the state would be done purely on a linguistic basis.[83]

Morarji Desai, Biju Patnaik and Ram Subhag Singh strongly opposed the resolution of the Congress Working Committee. They opposed the demand as communal. But Kamraj, the then President of the Congress Working Committee, carried the majority with him. He argued, "How can Punjabi be denied the benefit of the very national principle while the people of the other states were already enjoying the right to have life and work under their own linguistic state".[84] Y.B. Chavan, conscious of the Sikh's unqualified support in Indo-Pak war supported Kamraj. He observed, "A decision on the demand for a Punjabi state would not be delayed because of the geographical position of Punjab."[85]

Sant Fateh Singh expressed his gratification to the Congress Working Committee and hoped Hindu-Sikh unity in the proposed Punjabi Suba would persist. He said, "I am definitely opposed to Master Tara Singh's demand for independent Sikh State or for self-determined political status of the Sikhs. Our demand has been a Punjabi Suba as part of India. Bharat is my country and each particle of this land is sacred to me. How can we leave our home?"[86]

The Parliamentary Committee submitted its report on 18 March, 1966. It recommended that the Punjabi-speaking region be constituted into a unilingual Punjabi State, the Hindi-speaking region is formed into Haryana State and the hill areas of the erstwhile Punjab be merged with Himachal Pradesh. The recommendation was officially accepted on 21 March, 1966 by the Government of India and a Punjab Boundary Commission under the Chairmanship of Justice J.C. Shah with Subimal Datt and M.M. Philip as members, was appointed.[87]

The Commission was required to apply the linguistic principle with due regard to the census figures of 1961 and other relevant considerations and to take into consideration other factors such as :[88]

1. Administrative Convenience;
2. Economic Well-being;
3. Geographical Contiguity;
4. Facility of Communications.

The Commission submitted its report on the division of Punjab to the Central Government on 31 May, 1966. In its report, Commission reorganised the state by giving Hindi-speaking area to Haryana, Punjabi-speaking area to reorganised Punjab and hill areas (including Kangra and Shimla districts) to Himachal Pradesh. After minor modifications, the Shah Commission report was introduced as Punjab Reorganisation Bill (1966) and was approved by both houses of the Parliament in September, 1966.[89]

On 18 September, 1966, the Punjab Reorganisation Bill (1966) received the President's assent and Punjab was divided once again, this time into three parts. The new Punjab came into existence on 1 November, 1966 and comprised of the following areas; the districts of Gurdaspur, Hoshiarpur, Amritsar, Kapurthala, Jullundhar, Ferozepur, Bhatinda, Ludhiana, Patiala, Sangrur (excluding Narwana and Jind tehsil) and Ropar and Kharar tehsil of Ambala district.[90] It was decided by the Government of India that Chandigarh was to be Union Territory and the joint capital of both the states.

The Akalis reacted sharply and they put pressure on the Union Government for the inclusion of Chandigarh in Punjab. Akali leader Sant Fateh Singh issued a statement warning that the Government would be responsible for the consequences that might follow if Chandigarh went to Haryana.[91]

While in Haryana, the Punjab Reorganisation Act was welcomed, in Punjab it aroused the opposition of both the Sikhs and the Punjabi Hindus. The Punjabi Hindus opposed it because it had placed them in minority in the new state.[92] At the time of publication of the report; Sant Fateh Singh had gone abroad. Sant Fateh Singh on his return opposed the reorganisation. Sant claimed, "The Punjab Boundary Commission Report smacks of communalism" and further declared, "Chandigarh at no cost will be allowed to remain out of Punjabi Suba."[93]

Punjab was the jeweled crown of India at one time and its boundaries extended from Peshawar right up to the gates of Mathura. Those who had the good fortune of seeing the glory of Punjab had very sad day when it was cut down to eleven districts. The partition of the country in 1947 had already crippled Punjab. It limped on to resecure place of honour in the country. The 1966 partition impaired it beyond repairs for all times to come. What has been the gain? Only a sentimental victory of the Akali Dal that they got a Punjabi Suba with a majority of the Sikh population. In fact, many people, even from amongst the Sikhs and particularly those who did not see eye to eye with Sant Fateh Singh pointed it as a Punjabi Subee (feminine gender of Suba). S. Gurnam Singh, the first Akali Chief Minister of Punjab, who later fell out with Sant Fateh Singh published a booklet "Dictatorship and Revolt" recorded in Para 9 at page 4 at the booklet as follows :[94]

> "Every so called fast-unto-death and threat of self-immolation had led to further shrinkage of the Punjabi-speaking state because every time Sant embarks on an adventurous path, he makes an unfavourable bargain to save his life".

REFERENCES

1. B.R. Nayar : *Minority Politics in Punjab*, Princeton University, Princeton (1966), p. 280.
2. *Ibid.*, p. 281.
3. J.S. Garewal : *The Akalis : A Short History*, Punjab Studies Publication, Chandigarh (1996), p. 111.
4. *The Statesman*, 2 December, 1947.
5. *The Hindustan Times*, 21 September, 1947.
6. *Akali Patrika*, 11 October, 1949.
7. *The Tribune*, 12 November, 1949.
8. *Ibid.*

9. A.S. Sarhadi : *Punjabi Suba : The Story of the Struggle,* U.C. Kapoor and Sons, Delhi (1970), p. 203.

10. *Author Moore* was an English writer who had gone on fast-unto-death with Gandhiji in November 1947, when Gandhiji protested against the withdrawing of the certain amounts to Pakistan by the Indian Government.

11. A.S. Sarhadi : *Op. cit.,* p. 200.

12. *Ibid.,* p. 207.

13. *Ibid.,* pp. 209-10.

14. J.S. Garewal : *Op. cit.,* p. 113.

15. A.S. Sarhadi : *Op. cit.,* p. 221.

16. A.S. Narang : *Punjab Politics in National Perspetive,* Geetanjali Publishing House, New Delhi (1986), p. 130.

17. Devinder Pal Sandhu : *Sikhs in Indian Politics : Study of a Minority,* Patriot Publishers, New Delhi (1992), p. 160.

18. J.S. Garewal : *Op. cit.,* p. 123.

19. A.S. Narang : *Op. cit.,* p. 33.

20. A.S. Sarhadi : *Op. cit.,* p. 233.

21. Devinder Pal Sandhu : *Op. Cit.,* pp. 91-92.

22. Satya M. Rai : *Punjab Since Partition,* Durga Publications, Delhi (1986), p. 291.

23. Khushwant Singh : *A History of the Sikhs, 1839-1974,* Vol. II, Oxford University Press, Delhi (1966), p. 298.

24. *Report of the States Reorganisation Commission,* (1955), Manager, Government of India Press, New Delhi, Para 539, p. 146.

25. Satya M. Rai : *Op. cit.,* p. 291.

26. Harbans Singh : *The Heritage of the Sikhs,* Manohar, New Delhi (1983), p. 321.

27. K.C. Gulati : *The Akalis : Past and Present,* Ashajanak Publication, New Delhi (1974), p. 163.

28. Harbans Singh : *Op. cit.,* p. 322.

29. K.C. Gulati : *Op. cit.,* p. 163.

30. Mohan Lal : *Disintegration of Punjab,* Sameer Prakashan, Chandigarh (1984), pp. 26-27.

31. *Ibid.*, p. 28.
32. A.S. Narang : *Storm Over the Sutlej : The Akali Politics*, Geetanjali Publishing House, New Delhi (1983), p. 131.
33. A.S. Narang : *Op. cit.*, p. 37.
34. K.C. Gulati : *Op. cit.*, p. 166.
35. J.S. Grewal : *Op. cit.*, p. 129.
36. *Ibid.*
37. Harbans Singh : *Op. cit.*, p. 328.
38. J.S. Grewal : *Op. cit.*, p. 129.
39. K.C. Gulati : *Op. cit.*, p. 169.
40. A.S. Sarhadi : *Op. cit.*, p. 318-319.
41. K.C. Gulati : *Op. cit.*, p. 169.
42. J.S. Grewal : *Op. cit.*, p. 129.
43. K.C. Gulati : *Op. cit.*, p. 169.
44. A.S. Sarhadi : *Op. cit.*, p. 326.
45. A.S. Narang : *Op. cit.*, p. 154.
46. K.C. Gulati : *Op. cit.*, p. 170.
47. Gulshan Rai : *Formation of Haryana*, B.R. Publishing Corporation, Delhi (1987), p. 99.
48. A.S. Sarhadi : *Op. cit.*, p. 336.
49. Gulshan Rai : *Op. cit.*, p. 99.
50. A.S. Sarhadi : *Op. cit.*, p. 343-344.
51. K.C. Gulati : *Op. cit.*, p. 173.
52. Gulshan Rai : *Op. cit.*, p. 100.
53. Paul R. Brass : *Language, Religion and Politics in North India*, Cambridge University Press, Cambridge (1974), p. 321.
54. J.S. Grewal : *Op. cit.*, p. 131.
55. Khushwant Singh : *Op. cit.*, pp. 299-300.
56. *The Times of India*, Bombay, 2 October, 1961.
57. *The Hindu*, 1 November, 1961.
58. Gulshan Rai : *Op. cit.*, p. 103.
59. K.C. Gulati : *Op. cit.*, p. 176.
60. *The Times of India*, 10 February, 1961.

61. Gulshan Rai : *Op. cit.*, p. 104.
62. A.S. Narang : *Op. cit.*, p. 160.
63. J.S. Grewal : *Op. cit.*, p. 133.
64. A.S. Sarhadi : *Op. cit.*, p. 377.
65. *Ibid.*, p. 390.
66. Satya M. Rai : *Op. cit.*, p. 309.
67. A.S. Sarhadi : *Op. cit.*, p. 390.
68. *Ibid.*, p. 391.
69. *Ibid.*
70. Satya M. Rai : *Op. cit.*, p. 390.
71. A.S. Sarhadi : *Op. cit.*, pp. 394-95.
72. K.C. Gulati : *Op. cit.*, p. 180.
73. A.S. Sarhadi : *Op. cit.*, p. 398.
74. K.C. Gulati : *Op. cit.*, p. 180.
75. Gulshan Rai : *Op. cit.*, p. 117.
76. K.C. Gulati : *Op. cit.*, p. 180-81.
77. J.S. Grewal : *Op. cit.*, p. 136.
78. A.S. Sarhadi : *Op. cit.*, pp. 416-17.
79. Gulshan Rai : *Op. cit.*, p. 120.
80. K.C. Gulati : *Op. cit.*, p. 181.
81. Gulshan Rai : *Op. cit.*, p. 128.
82. Mohan Lal : *Op. cit.*, p. 319.
83. *Ibid.*, p. 320.
84. P.C. Joshi : *"Triumph of a Just Cause Punjabi Suba : A Symposium"*, National Book Club, New Delhi, n.d., p. 82.
85. *The Hindustan Times*, 10 March, 1966.
86. A.S. Sarhadi : *Op. cit.*, p. 449.
87. Satya M. Rai : *Op. cit.*, p. 311.
88. *Punjab Boundary Commission Report*, Manager Government of India Press, Delhi, (1966), Appendix IV, p. 60.
89. Satya M. Rai : *Op. cit.*, p. 312.
90. *Ibid.*, p. 314.

91. *The Statesman,* 10 June, 1966.
92. J.C. Anand : *"Punjab Politics of Retreating Communalism"* in Iqbal Narain (ed.) : *State Politics in India,* Meenakshi Prakashan, Meerut (1976), p. 276.
93. *The Hindu,* 23 September, 1966.
94. Mohan Lal : *Op. cit.,* pp. 323-24.

6

Summing Up

The growth of various secular minded organisations such as the 'Indian Association', 'All India Political Conference' etc. culminated in the birth of the Indian National Congress in 1885. The moving spirit behind the formation of the Congress was A.O. Hume. After closely following the trend of events in the late nineteenth century, Hume realised that "the cure for unrest lay in the foundation of a genuine nationalist movement". With this idea in mind Hume formed the Indian National Congress.

The birth of the Indian National Congress was an unprecedented phenomenon in the political history of India. The Congress was the central organ of the new society, which had evolved as a result of economic, social and cultural changes taking shape during the hundred years since Plassey. In 1885, the future of the Congress was difficult to forecast. Like all institutions of such a type, it had to pass through rough times and through periods of indifference of the people and of disfavour of the Government, before it became the powerful instrument, which challenged the might of the British Empire.

The sessions of the Congress in the early years were conducted in a decent, sober and rather subdued spirit. There was no revolutionary fervour in the resolutions or the speeches. Moderation was their keynote. The presidential addresses recounted the benefits of British rule, contained assurances of India's loyalty to the crown and reiterated India's desire to remain within the British Empire.

The Congress under the leadership of the Indian Liberals

from 1885-1905 fought for administrative reforms such as the separation of judicial and executive functions, the right of the Indians to be admitted to public services on equal terms and subsequently for the Indianisation of services, for the rescinding of the Arms Act, against the economic drain which engendered poverty of the Indian people and heavy military expenditure.

The Government enacted section 124(A) and 153(A) in 1897 to combat the Congress activities. Secret Press Committees were established in 1898 restricting the freedom of the press. Lord Curzon wrote in 1900 to the Secretary of State "The Congress is tottering to its fall and one of my great ambitions while in India is to assist it to a peaceful demise."

The non-fulfillment of the most important of their demands gave impetus to the growth of militant nationalism in India. The militant nationalists drew inspiration from India's past, evoked the great episodes in the history of the Indian people and tried to infuse national pride and self-respect among them. They criticized the idealising of the western and especially British culture by the liberals as cultural capitulation to the British rulers. The militant nationalists asserted that this would engender an inferiority complex among the Indians and suppress their national pride and self-confidence so vital to the struggle for freedom.

Freedom movement in India took definite shape and form between the years 1905 to 1919. This period was marked by agitation known as anti-partition of Bengal, emergence of terroism, the birth of Muslim league, its hostility and reconciliation with the Congress, a temporary split within the Congress, the eclipse of moderates and the Home Rule Movement. It is interesting to note that "the nationalist movement became less provincial and less religious, its adherents more interested in their status as Indian. At the same time, the leaders of the freedom movement became increasingly revolutionary and independent.".

The First World War broke out in Europe in 1914. After the war, the British Government granted some concessions in the form of 1919 Act. The main features of this act were

Dyarchy in provinces, enlarged Viceroy's executive council and bicameral legislature in the Centre. But the Congress condemned the proposals of the Act as "disappointing, unsatisfactory and inadequate". The Act of 1919 caused widespread discontent in India. The Government tried to suppress the discontent by passing the Rowlatt Act. It provided for arrest and trial without a show of normal legal procedure.

As protest to this Act, Gandhi organised a countrywide passive resistance movement. He called for a complete 'hartal' to mark the people's sense of resentment. In Punjab, there were riots and casualities caused by police firing in many cities. Meanwhile, the local Congress had already announced a meeting at Jallianwala Bagh for Baisakhi fair. As soon as General Dyer received news of the meeting, he marched a platoon of infantry to Jallianwala Bagh. He occupied the only entrance and without giving any warning to the people to disperse, opened fire on the innocent people. Some 400 Indians were left dead and 1200 wounded. The Jallianwala Bagh massacre was indeed a dark tragedy.

The years between 1920 to 1947 is known as the last phase of India's freedom movement. The most striking point in the period is that the freedom movement was transformed into people's movement for liberty. On 1 August, 1920, Gandhi launched the historic Non-Cooperation Movement. The Non-Cooperation Movement included the surrender of titles, honorary offices, boycott of Government educational institutions, law courts and foreign goods. Non-violence was declared to be its integral part.

At a special session of the Indian National Congress called under the Presidentship of Lala Lajpat Rai on 4 September, 1920, an appeal was made to public servants to disassociate themselves from the administration and Government educational institutions and to boycott councils and foreign textiles.

As a result of non-cooperation call of Gandhi, students of educational institutions in Punjab went on a strike. Swadeshi was propagated and the boycott of foreign cloth was encouraged. The women also took part in the movement. The

Hindu-Muslim unity was one of the noteworthy features of the non-cooperation movement in Punjab. The role of the working class was equally noteworthy. The unity among the three communities totally upset the Punjab Administration.

Meanwhile, the Government announced that the general elections to Legislative Councils would be held in December 1920 under the reform scheme. However, the All India Congress Committee had given a call to boycott the elections of Provincial Legislative Councils and a number of Congress members withdrew from the Legislative Council elections in Punjab also. The impact of this boycott was far reaching on the minds of the votes. On 24 April, 1926, the ban on the Congress and the Khilafat was lifted, when the elections to the third Legislative Council were drawing near. Such a ban was also lifed from S.G.P.C. and the Akali Dal on 13 September, 1926.

In November 1927, the Simon Commission was appointed to enquire into the working of Reforms of 1919 and to make recommendations. The all India Congress Committee in its Madras Session passed a resolution to boycott the Simon Commission. Similarly, the All India Muslim League and the Hindu Mahasabha also resolved to boycott the Commission. Its visit was greeted with black flags and the cry of "Simon, Go back," and mass demonstration by the Congressmen and the Akalis. It was on this occasion that in Lahore, Lala Lajpat Rai was assaulted and beaten on his chest, which resulted in his death on 17 November, 1928. The death of Lala Lajpat Rai aroused a wave of indignation against British Government.

In 1930, the Congress launched the Civil Disobedience Movement and issued a call to boycott the Legislative Assemblies and the Councils. In March 1930, Gandhiji started his famous 'Dandi' march to protest against the notorious salt tax. In Punjab vigorous propaganda was conducted in favour of swadeshi and the boycott of the foreign cloth. The Government declared the provincial Congress Committee and all local Committees as unlawful bodies under the Criminal Law Amendment Act.

The Communal Award and the White Paper continued to

be the central theme of the Punjab politics for many years. Meanwhile, the Joint Select Committee of both the Houses of British Parliament recommended the British Government to pass the Indian Act of 1935. The new Act proposed a federal government at the Centre and provincial governments in the eleven provinces with a large measure of autonomy. The stage had been set for the elections in Punjab in 1937. After the elections, the Unionist party formed the Government under Sikander Hyat Khan. Sunder Singh Majithia, the leader of the Khalsa National Party joined the new ministry.

The Akalis who had been involved in the Shahid Ganj agitation felt perturbed over the Punjab Premier joining League due to Muslim domination in Punjab. To counteract the Muslim League's influences, the Shiromani Akali Dal's executive passed a resolution, exhorting Sikh masses to join the Indian National Congress. The pact between them brought the Akalis and the Congress leaders formally closer to one another.

After the outbreak of the Second World War in 1939, there was a wild talk of disbanding the Sikh force. The Congress ministries resigned in the seven provinces. In 1942, the World War took a significant turn, when Japanese Army was scoring success. It became necessary for the Viceroy as well as British Government to break the political deadlock in India. British War Cabinet sent Stafford Cripps to win over Indian support for the War. The Congress Working Committee in its resolution turned down the Cripps proposals, because of the novel principles of non-accession for a province. Gandhi described the Cripps proposals as "post dated cheque upon a crashing bank."

In the wake of Cripps mission's failure, the Indian National Congress launched the Quit India Movement. Mahatma Gandhi and all leading Congressmen were arrested. The Congress party was declared illegal. Then followed protests and spontaneous demonstrations all over the country.

In Punjab only some urban Hindus supported the movement. Propaganda among students, Hindus, Muslims, Sikhs was carried out through bulletins published in different languages. Woman participated in the movement. Strikes took place in the various educational institutions. But generally the Quit India Movement in Punjab was feeble.

Meanwhile, World War-II came to an end and the British Government sought to reach at some solution to the Indian Problem. After several meetings with the leaders of the Congress, Muslim League and the Sikhs, Cabinet Mission issued on 16 May, 1946, a statement envisaging confederal scheme for India, giving defence, foreign affairs and communication to the Centre and all other powers to the states. Then on 20 February, 1947, the British Prime Minister Atlee made historic announcement. It stated that the British would quit India not later than June 1948. On July 19, 1947 the British Parliament provided for the end of the British rule and the partition of India on 15 August. On 14 and 15 August, 1947, Pakistan and India came into existence.

The partition of Punjab brought about the most radical change in the life of this region since the fall of the Sikh empire and the annexation by the British. It came as a culminating point of social, economic and political upheavals of nearly half a century and as a result of the sectarian and partisan intrigues of the parties concerned. The division, however, did not solve the communal problem, for it could not perform the miracle of bringing about a complete reconciliation of the old feuds. On the contrary, in its wake cropped up a lot of other problems, which necessitated the immediate attention of all concerned. It is nevertheless, a glorious tribute to the people of Punjab, that they fought adversities with fortitude and with a miraculous speed only in a decade resettled in various kinds of professions.

Punjab, which was crucial to any scheme of partition of the country, became the worst victim of violence subsequent to the acceptance of the division of India and the province itself. As a consequence, almost the total non-Muslim population from the West Punjab and an overwhelming majority of the Muslims in the East Punjab left their homeland to join their co-religionists on the other side of the border.

The problems that came up as a result of the migration of millions of people and the heroic manner in which the brave Punjabis faced them forms another glorious chapter in the history of the heroic tradition of the people of the Punjab.

The East Punjab Government was organised with a temporary capital at Shimla with Gopi Chand Bhargava as its first Chief Minister. After the partition of Punjab in 1947, half a million non-Muslim refugees poured into East Punjab and East Punjab States. Their rehabilitation at different places in the Union was the biggest problem faced by the Government immediately after the formation of Patiala and East Punjab States Union (Pepsu) with Maharaja Yadvindra Singh as Rajpramukh and Gian Singh Rarewala as Chief Minister.

The Pepsu being the nearest to the border attracted a sizeable number of refugees. They had brought a legacy of pain, agitation and nervous tension. The task of rehabilitation of these grief-stricken uprooted people at a time when the administration was showing signs of complete breakdown added to the complexities of the problem. The exigencies of the circumstances compelled the Government to take up certain important measures to stabilise and rehabilitate these displaced persons. As an interim measure, refugee camps were set up in several towns and localities, where the refugees were provided with free food, shelter and clothing.

The partition of Punjab shook the administrative, economic and political machinery of the province to its foundations and brought into its wake a host of complicated problems. The problems were so inter-linked that the aggravation of one complicated the other, although it is difficult to say whether the solution of one tangle could lead to the unknotting of the other.

One of the linguistic state demand which has been of major significance in Indian politics in the post-independence period is that made by the Shiromani Akali Dal on behalf of the Sikh community for the creation of Punjabi Suba, or Punjabi-speaking state, by the exclusion of certain Hindi-speaking areas from the existing state of Punjab. The demand has been made in the name of the Punjabi language, but the real purpose is believed to be the formation of a Sikh majority state, which would be under the political control of the Akali Dal.

The Government of India constituted States Reorganisation Commission in 1953. The Akali Dal in its memorandum urged the formation of Punjabi Suba or a Punjabi-speaking state by joining together the Punjabi-speaking areas of Punjab, Pepsu and Rajasthan. The Commission rejected the Akalis demand. On the other hand, the Punjab Government advocated the formation of the Greater Punjab (Maha Punjab), which was more or less on the same line as suggested by the Hindu organisations.

After the rejection of the Punjabi Suba demand, the Akali launched an agitation to achieve their goal. The Government tried to contain the Akali agitation by offering the Regional Formula, which had to certain extent, accepted the principle of division of Punjab. The Akali Dal suspended the agitation and decided to merge with the Congress for contesting the 1957 assembly elections.

The Regional Plan was met with severe opposition from the Hindu sectarian groups and parties. The Government too was reluctant to implement it honestly on account of opposition from within. Faced with the opposition from Hindu communal sections and unwillingness of the Punjab Government to enhance the status of Punjabi language, the Akalis once again renewed the demand for Punjabi Suba and launched a movement in its support from May 1960. The Government took pre-emptive action and arrested Master Tara Singh.

Sant Fateh Singh, the Vice-President of Shiromani Akali Dal emerged as a leader of the rural Sikhs with a solid base amongst the Jat peasantry. Sant emphasized more on language than religious basis. He continued the struggle and launched large-scale morcha. But the Central leadership remained firm on the stand that Punjabi Suba could not be formed. Sant Fateh Singh undertook a fast-unto-death on 18 December, 1960. However, on the advice of Master Tara Singh, he gave his twenty-two days fast to negotiate the matter with the Prime Minister.

The Prime Minister Nehru remained resolutely opposed to the creation of a Punjabi Suba until the end of his life. Partap Singh Kairon had dominated Punjab politics from 1956 till 1964, the period in which he had the backing of Nehru. He strongly opposed the creation of a Punjabi-speaking state on political consideration, as he feared that the Congress would go out of office in Punjab and that his political career would suffer a setback if Punjabi-speaking state was created. However, Jawaharlal Nehru died on 27 May, 1964. Partap Singh Kairon resigned from the Punjab Chief Ministership on 14 June, 1964 in the wake of his indictment by Das Commission. It was then that the anti-Punjabi Suba front weakened.

With the change of leadership at the Centre due to the death of Jawaharlal Nehru in 1964, there was a sea change in the thinking pattern of the new leadership and bureaucracy regarding the demand of Punjabi Suba. Soon after the announcement of the cease-fire, the Union Home Minister Nanda announced the creation of cabinet sub-committee consisting of Mr. Indira Gandhi, Y.B. Chavan and Mahavir Tyagi, which would, from time to time, advise the Parliamentary Committee to be set up with Hukam Singh, Speaker, as its president. The Home Minister expressed his confidence that the deliberations of these committees would lead to a satisfactory solution of the question.

The situation on the issue was still fluid when news came of the death of Lal Bahadur Shastri at Tashkent. Mrs. Indira Gandhi was elected leader of the party and Prime Minister on January 20, 1966. She wrote a letter soon after to Sant Fateh Singh and assured the Akali leader that Government was more anxious to solve the issue as early as possible. After the Indo-Pak war of 1965, the Government of India set up Punjab Boundary Commission on 23 April, 1966, to reorganise the Punjab on linguistic basis. It submitted its report on the division of the Punjab to the Government on 31 May, 1966. The Reorganisation of Punjab Bill was enacted by Parliament in September 1966. The Punjabi-speaking State Punjab was inaugurated on 1 November, 1966.

Appendices

APPENDIX—I

Sachar Formula

In October 1949, a language formula known as the Sachar Formula was adopted by the Punjab Government. This formula enunciated that :

1. Hindi and Punjabi are both recognised as regional languages of the province.
2. Punjabi shall be the medium of instruction in Punjabi-speaking area in all schools up to the matriculation stage and Hindi shall be taught as a compulsory subject from the last class of the primary department, and up to the matriculation stage, but in case of girls schools up to the middle class only. Likewise, Hindi shall be the medium of instruction in the Hindi-speaking area in all schools up to the matriculation stage and Punjabi shall be taught as a compulsory language from the last class of the primary department and up to the matriculation stage, but in the case of girls schools up to the middle classes only.
3. There will, however, be cases where the parent or guardian of a pupil may wish him/her to get instruction in Hindi in the Punjabi-speaking area and in Punjabi in Hindi-speaking area on the ground that Hindi/Punjabi and not the regional language is his/her mother tongue. In such cases, without questioning that declaration of the parent or guardian, arrangements will be made for instructions in Hindi/Punjabi during the primary stage provided there are not fewer than 40 pupils in the whole school wishing to be instructed in Hindi/Punjabi or 10 such pupils in the primary stage

but the regional languages from the fourth class in the case of boys schools and sixth class in the case of girls' schools. In the secondary stage also the medium of instruction for pupils described in this paragraph will be Hindi/Punjabi if 1/3rd of the total number of pupils in a Government, Municipal or District Board School request for instruction in Hindi/Punjabi, Government will also require aided schools to arrange for instruction in Hindi/Punjabi if desired by 1/3rd of pupils provided that there are no adequate facilities for instruction in Hindi/Punjabi in the area. If this condition of 1/3rd is not satisfied, then, regional language as medium of instruction in the secondary stage. Hindi-speaking and Punjabi-speaking pupils will be given the option of answering questions in Hindi/ Punjabi for the first two years of the secondary stage. The regional language would, however, be a compulsory subject of study throughout the secondary stage.

4. To meet an unforeseen situation arising out of the demand for imparting education in a medium other than the regional language, the government may issue further directions by way of necessary modifications.

5. In an unaided recognised school, the medium of instruction will be determined by the management. It will not be obligatory on it to provide facilities for instruction in any other medium, but it will be incumbent on it to provide for the teaching of Punjabi or Hindi; as the case may be, as a second language.

6. These proposals do not apply to those pupils whose mother tongue is neither Punjabi nor Hindi. Suitable arrangements will be made for the education of such pupils in their mother tongue if there are a sufficient number of such pupils at one place to make this arrangement possible.

APPENDIX—II

Instrument of Accession

Whereas by Instrument of Accession executed in August

1947, the Rulers of the State specified in the Schedule hereto have acceded to the Dominion of India;

And whereas by Covenant entered into in May 1948, the Rulers of the said States have with the consent of the Government of India agreed to the integration of their respective territories into a single State known as to the United State of..........in this instrument referred to as "the United State;"

And whereas it is expedient that a fresh Instrument of Accession should be executed on behalf of the United State replacing the Instrument of Accession executed in August, 1947, by the Rulers of the said State and accepting as matters with respect to which the Dominion Legislature may make laws for the United State all matters mentioned in List I and List III of the Seventh Schedule to the Government of India Act, 1935, except matters relating to taxation;

Now, therefore, I Maharajadhiraja Rajeshwar Sir Yadvindera Singh Mahindar Bahadur of Patiala, *Rajpramukh* of the Patiala and East Punjab States Union do hereby execute this Instrument of Accession for and one behalf of the United State, and

1. I hereby declare that accede to the Dominion of India with the intent that the Governor General of India, the Dominion Legislature, the Federal Court and any other Dominion authority established for the purpose of the Dominion shall, by virtue of this Instrument of Accession but subject always to the terms thereof, and for the purpose only of the Dominion, exercise in relation to the United State such functions as may be vested in them by or under the Government of India Act, 1935, as for the time being in force in the Dominion of India.

2. I hereby assume the obligation of ensuring that the effect is given to the provisions of the Act within the United State so far as they are applicable therein by virtue of this Instrument of Accession.

3. I accept all matters enumerated in List I and List III of the Seventh Schedule to the Act as matters in respect of which the Dominion Legislature may make laws for the United State.
4. I hereby declare that I accede to the Dominion of India on the assurance that if an agreement is made between the Governor General and the Rajpramukh of the United State whereby any functions in relation to the administration in the United State of any law of the Dominion Legislative shall be exercised by the Rajpramukh, then any such agreement shall be deemed to form part of this instrument and shall be constructed and effect accordingly.
5. I further declare that the provisions contained in Part VI of the Act with respect to interference with water supplies shall apply in relation to the United State.
6. The terms of this Instrument of Accession shall not be varied by any amendment of the Act or of the Indian Independence Act, 1947, unless such amendment is accepted by the Rajpramukh of the United State by an Instrument supplementary to this Instrument.
7. Nothing in this Instrument shall empower the Dominion Legislature to make any law for the United State authorising the compulsory acquisition of land for any purpose, but should the Dominion for the purpose of a Dominion Law which applies in the United State deem it necessary to acquire any land the Rajpramukh of the United State shall at the request and at the expense of the Dominion Government acquire the land or if the land belongs to the United State transfer it to them on such terms as may be agreed, or in default of agreement determined by an arbitrator to be appointed by the Chief Justice of India.
8. Nothing in this Instrument shall be deemed to commit the United State in any way to acceptance of any future constitution of India or to father the discretion of the Government of the United State to enter into

arrangements with the Government of India under any such future constitution.

9. Save as provided by or under this Instrument nothing contained in this Instrument shall affect the exercise of any powers, authority and rights enjoyed by the Rajpramukh or the validity of any law for the time being in force in the United State or any part thereof.

10. The Instruments of Accession executed in August 1947 by the rulers of the States specified in the schedule hereto is hereby cancelled.

Given under my hands this 7th August, 1948.

Yadvindra Singh
Rajpramukh

I do hereby accept this Instrument of Accession.

Dated—13 September, 1948

Sd/-
C. Rajgopalachari
Governor General of India

Schedule

1. Faridkot	5. Nabha
2. Jind	6. Patiala
3. Kapurthala	7. Kalsia
4. Malerkotla	8. Nalagarh

Source : Patiala and East Punjab States Since Inauguration, issued by Pepsu Government, Patiala (1951), pp. 70-73

APPENDIX—III

Regional Plan

Outline of the Regional Committees in the Punjab.

1. There will be one legislature for the whole of the recognised state of the Punjab, which will be sole lawmaking body for the entire State, and there will be one Governor for the State, aided and advised by Council of Ministers responsible to the State Assembly for the entire field of administration.

2. For the more convenient transaction of the business of Government with regard to some specified matters, the State will be divided into two regions, namely, the Punjabi-speaking and the Hindi-speaking regions.
3. For each region there will be a regional committee of the State Assembly consisting of the members of the State Assembly belonging to each region including the Ministers for that region but not including the Chief Minister.
4. Legislation relating to specified matters will be referred to the Regional Committees. In respect of specified matters proposals may also be made by the Regional Committees to the State Government for legislation or with regard to question of general policy not involving any financial commitment other than expenditure of a routine and incidental character.
5. The advice tendered by the Regional Committees will normally be accepted by the Government and the State Legislature. In case of difference of opinion, reference will be made to the Governor whose decision will be final and binding.
6. The Regional Committees will deal with the following matters :
    - *(i)* Development and economic planning, within the framework of the general development plans and policies formulated by the State Legislature;
    - *(ii)* Local Self-Government, that is to say, the constitutional powers of municipal corporation, improvement trusts, district boards and other local authorities for the purpose of local self-government of village administration including Panchayats;
    - *(iii)* Public Health and Sanitation, local hospitals and dispensaries;
    - *(iv)* Primary and Secondary education;

(v) Agriculture;

(vi) Cottage and small-scale industries;

(vii) Preservation, Protection and improvement of stock and prevention of animal diseases, veterinary training and practice;

(viii) Ponds and prevention of cattle trespass;

(ix) Protection of wild animals and birds;

(x) Fisheries;

(xi) Inns and innkeepers;

(xii) Markets and fairs;

(xiii) Co-operative societies; and

(xiv) Charities and charitable institutions charitable and religious endowments and religious institutions.

7. Provision will be made under the appropriate Central Statute to empower the President to constitute regional committees and to make provision in the rules of business of Government and the rules of procedure of the Legislative Assembly in order to give effect to the arrangements outlined in the preceding paragraphs. The provisions made in the rules of business and procedure for the proper functioning of regional committees will not be alerted without the approval of the President.

8. The demarcation of the Hindi and Punjabi regions in the proposed Punjab State will be done in consultation with the State Government and the other interests concerned.

9. The Sachar Formula will continue to operate in the area comprised in the existing Punjab State and in the area now comprised in the Pepsu State, the existing arrangements will continue until they are replaced or altered by agreement later.

10. The official language of each region will, at the district

level and below, be the respective regional language.

11. The State will be bilingual recognising both Punjabi (in Gurmukhi script) and Hindi (in Devnagari script) as the official languages of the State.
12. The Punjab Government will establish two separate departments for developing Punjabi and Hindi languages.
13. The general safeguards proposed for linguistic minorities will be applicable to the Punjab like other States.
14. In accordance with and in furtherance of its policy to promote the growth of all regional languages, the Central Government will encourage the development of Punjabi language.

Source : "Papers Relating to Hindi Agitation in Punjab," Chandigarh : Public Relations Department, Punjab (1957), pp. 9-10.

APPENDIX—IV

Number of Seats and Percentage of Votes Polled by Political Parties, 1952-1962

Political Party	*1952 Seats Won/ Percentage*	*1957 Seats Won/ Percentage*	*1962 Seats Won/ Percentage*
1	*2*	*3*	*4*
Congress	60/31.3%	71/48.6%	49/45.7%
Forward Bloc	1/2.2%	-/-	-/-
Akali Dal	31/24%	-/-	19/20.7%
Jan Sangh	-/4%	5/7.2%	4/7.6%
PSP	-/3.4%	-/0.9%	-/0.7%
Scheduled Caste Federation	1/3.8%	1/6.2%	-/-
CPI	6/6.1%	3/17.7%	9/9.8%

(Contd.)

(Contd.)

1	*2*	*3*	*4*
CP (L)	2/2.1%	-/-	-/-
Swatantra Party (Founded in 1959)	-/-	-/-	-/2.4%
Unsuccessful Parties and Independents	9/23.1%	6/19.4%	5/10.3%

Source : Election Commission of India, Compiled from Baxter, *District Voting Trends in India,* pp. 235-236.

Bibliography

1. PRIMARY SOURCES

A. Unpublished Sources

*(a) **Proceeding of the Government of India*** (available at the National Archives of India, New Delhi)

Ministry of Home Affairs, File Nos. 53/69/53 (Public) : 1953

Home Department (Political) Files

File Nos;

• 80, 82, 83, 85, 90, 93 and 95	1919
• 106	1921
• 952	1924
• 138/26	1926
• 542/21	1926
• 65	1930
• 15/IV	1930
• 18/X	1930
• 201/40	1930
• 16/X	1930
• 5/45	1931
• 18/3	1931
• 41/1	1932
• 4/9	1937
• 18/4/90	1940
• 3/16	1942
• 79 (Vol. III)	1946

Home Department Political (B), Proceeding nos;

- 80, 82, 83, 85 1919
- 90, 93, 95 1919
- 59 1920

(b) ***Private Papers :*** Available at the National Archives of India, New Delhi :

- Gian Singh Rarewala Papers

Available at the Nehru Memorial Museum and Library, New Delhi :

- All India Congress Committee Papers
- Hindu Mahasabha Papers
- Moti Lal Nehru Papers

(c) ***Recorded Interview :*** Available at the Nehru Memorial Museum and Library, New Delhi.

- Gurmukh Singh Musafir
- Ishar Singh Majhail
- Ujjal Singh
- Hukam Singh
- Feroze Chand

Available at the Oral History Cell of Department of the Punjab Historical Studies, Punjabi University, Patiala.

- Giani Kartar Singh
- Bhim Sen Sachar
- Gian Singh Rarewala
- Ajit Singh Sarhadi
- Hukam Singh

B. Published Sources

(a) Official Records

- Bhide, M.R. : *Progress of Rehabilitation in Patiala and East Punjab States Union,* Patiala, 1951.
- Malhotra, V.P. : *Economic Condition of Displaced Persons Settled in East Punjab,* Shimla, 1950.

- Government of India, *Report of the States Reorganisation Commission,* Delhi, 1955.
- Patiala Relief and Rehabilitation Committee, *Report of the Working of the Relief and Rehabilitation Committee of Patiala State,* Patiala, 1948.
- Government of India, *White Papers on Indian States,* Delhi, 1950.
- *Patiala and East Punjab States Union Since Inauguration,* a publication of Director of Information and Public Relations, Pepsu Government. Patiala, 1951.
- *Punjab Public Relations Department,* Punjab, Chandigarh, 1956.
- *Facts About Pepsu,* Directorate of Information and Public Relations, Patiala, 1953.
- *Millions on the Move,* Publication Division, Government of India, Delhi, 1948.

(a) *Historical Background of Pepsu,* A State Government Publication, Patiala, 1952.

  - Mohan Singh : *Report on the Working of Relief,* Patiala.
  - Nair, L.R. (ed.) : *Rural Rehabilitation in East Punjab, 1947-48,* Shimla, 1948.
  - *Papers Relating to Hindi Agitation in Punjab,* Public Relations Department, Chandigarh, 1957.
  - *Sidelines on Akali Strategy,* Public Relations Department, Chandigarh, 1961.
  - *Report on the First General Elections in India, 1951-52,* Election Commission, New Delhi, 1955.
  - *Report on the States Reorganisation Commission,* Manager, Government of India Press, 1955.
  - *Report on the Second General Election in India, 1957,* Election Commission, New Delhi, 1959.
  - *Report on the Third General Elections in India 1962,* Election Commission, New Delhi, 1963.
  - *The Punjab Reorganisation Act, 1966,* Manager of

Publications, Government of India Press, Delhi, 1967.

- *Punjab Boundary Commission Report,* Manager, Government of India Press, Delhi, 1966.

(b) Debates

- Punjab Legislative Assembly Debates, Lahore, 1921.
- Punjab Legislative Assembly Debates, Chandigarh, 1954.
- Pepsu Vidhan Sabha Debates, 1955.
- Lok Sabha Debates on the Report of the States Reorganisation Commission, Lok Sabha, Secretariat, New Delhi, 1956.

(b) Collection of Documents, Letters and Speeches

- Banerjee, A.C. (ed.) : *Indian Constitutional Documents, 1917-39,* Delhi, 1949.
- Chopra, P.N. (ed.) : *Quit India Movement,* New Delhi, 1976.
- Dass, Durga (ed.) : *Sardar Patel's Correspondence, 1945-50,* Vol. I-X, Ahmedabad, 1971—74.
- Government of India : *Jawaharlal Nehru's Speeches,* Vols. I—V, Ministry of Information and Broadcasting New Delhi, 1949—68.
- Gopal, S. (ed.) : *Selected Works of Jawaharlal Nehru,* Vol. I-XV, New Delhi, 1972—82.
- Mitra, H.N. and Mitra, N.N. (ed.) : *Indian Annual Register,* Calcutta, 1920—47.
- Narayan, Sriram (ed.) : *The Selected Works of Mahatma Gandhi,* Vol. I—V, Ahmedabad, 1962—68.
- Pandey, B.N. (ed.) : *The Indian Nationalist Movement, 1885—1947,* Delhi, 1979.
- Gandhi, M.K. : *The Collected Works of Mahatma Gandhi,* Vol. I—XXXXII, Ahmedabad, 1968.

(c) Reports of Indian National Congress

- Report of the First Indian National Congress Session, Bombay, 1885.
- Report of the Fifteenth Indian National Congress Session, Lucknow, 1899.
- Report of the Twenty Fifth Indian National Congress Session, Lahore, 1909.
- Report of the Sixteenth Indian National Congress Session, Lahore, 1900.
- Report of the Thirty First Indian National Congress Session, Lucknow, 1916.
- Report of the Thirty Third Indian National Congress Session, Delhi, 1918.

(d) ***Ijlas-I-Khas*** (Available at the Punjab State Archives, Patiala)

- S. No. 2040, B. No. : 25/171
- S. No. 2042, B. No. : 25/171

(e) ***Punjab History Conference Proceedings*** (Published by the Department of Punjab Historical Studies, Punjabi University, Patiala).

- Mohinder Singh : *Akalis and the Non-Cooperation,* Patiala, 1978.

(f) ***The Punjab Past and Present*** (Bi-Annual Journal, Published by the Department of Punjab Historical Studies, Punjabi University, Patiala)

- Vol. XVI, Part-II, 1982
- Vol. XX, Part-II, 1986

C. Newspapers

- The Tribune (Ambala, Chandigarh, Lahore)
- National Herald (New Delhi)
- Akali Patrika (Jullundhar)
- The Hindustan Times (New Delhi)

- The Spokesman (New Delhi)
- The Times of India (New Delhi)
- The Hindu (Madras)
- Prabhat (New Delhi)
- Indian Express (New Delhi)
- The Hindustan Standard (Calcutta)
- Aftab-i-Punjab (Lahore)
- The People (Lahore)
- The Akali Te Pardesi (Amritsar)
- Leader (Allahabad)
- Pioneer (Lucknow)
- The Akali (Amritsar, Lahore)

2. SECONDARY SOURCES

- Adirayu, V.R. : *Sikh and India : Identity Crisis,* Hyderabad, 1991.
- Ahluwalia, M.M : *Freedom Struggle in India (1858—1909)* Delhi, 1965.
- Alexander, Horace : *New Citizens of India,* Oxford, 1951.
- Amrik Singh (ed.) : *Punjab in Indian Politics : Issues and Trends,* Delhi, 1985.
- Andrewes and Mukharjee : *Rise and Growth of Congress,* Meerut, 1967.
- Anup Chand Kaur : *The Punjab Crisis,* Delhi, 1985.
- Arora, S.C. : *Turmoil in Punjab Politics,* New Delhi, 1990.
- Azad, Maulana Abul Kalam : *India Wins Freedom,* Bombay, 1959.
- Bhatnagar, R.P. : *The Rise and Growth of Hindi Journalism,* Allahabad, 1947.
- Bhide, M.R. : *Progress of Rehabilitation in PEPSU,* Patiala, 1951.

- Banerjee, A.C. : *Indian Constitutional Documents,* Calcutta, 1961.
- Brass, Paul R. : *Language, Religion and Politics in North India,* Cambridge, 1974.
- Chand, Tara : *History of the Freedom Movement in India,* Vol. II, New Delhi, 1972.
- Chandra, Bipan, Amales Tripathi and Barun De : *Freedom Struggle,* New Delhi, 1972.
- Chandra Prakash : *History of the Indian National Movement,* New Delhi, 1997.
- Chirol, Valentine : *India : Old and New,* London, 1926.
- Chopra, P.N., Ram Gopal and M.C. Bhargava : *A Century of the Indian National Congress (1885—1985),* Delhi, 1986.
- Chunni Lal, Lallubhai Parekh (ed.) : *Essays, Speeches, Addresses and Writings of Dadabhai Noiroji,* Bombay, 1987.
- Coupland, Reginald : *The Indian Problem,* New York, 1944.
- Dalip Singh : *Dynamics of Punjab Politics,* New Delhi, 1990.
- Darling, Malcolm : *The Punjab Peasant in Prosperity and Debt,* Delhi, 1977.
- Das, Durga (ed.) : *Sardar Patel's Correspondence, 1945—50,* Vol. IV, Ahmedabad, 1972.
- Desai, A.R. : *Social Background of Indian Nationalism,* Bombay, 1948.
- Dhanki, J.S. : *Lala Lajpat Rai and Indian Nationalism,* Jullundhar, 1990.
- Dodewell, H.H. : *A Sketch of the History of India from 1858 to 1918,* London, 1925.
- Dutt, K. Ịshwara : *Congress Encyclopedia,* Vol. I, New Delhi, 1941.
- Durlab Singh : *The Valiant Fighter,* Lahore, 1942.
- Fateh Singh : *Facts About Punjabi Suba,* Amritsar, 1960.

- Grewal, J. S. : *The Akalis : A Short History,* Chandigarh, 1996.
- Garewal J. S. : *The New Cambridge History of India, The Sikhs of the Punjab,* Cambridge, 1990.
- Ghose, Shankar : *Congress Presidential Speeches,* Delhi, 1977.
- Grover, D.R. : *Civil Disobedience Movement in Punjab, 1930—34,* Delhi, 1987.
- Gopal, S. : *Selected Works of Jawaharlal Nehru,* New Delhi, 1965.
- Gulati, K.C. : *The Akalis : Past and Present,* New Delhi, 1974.
- Gupta, D.C. : *National Movement and Constitutional Development,* Delhi, 1970.
- Gupta, Tara Chand : *Nine Months of Popular Ministry in PEPSU, Congressmen, What Now?* Patiala, 1949.
- Gurmit Singh : *History of the Sikh Struggle,* Delhi, 1991.
- Gursharan Singh : *History of PEPSU,* Delhi 1991.
- Harbans Singh (e) : *Essays in Honour of Dr. Ganda Singh,* Patiala, 1976.
- Harbans Singh (ed.) : *The Heritage of the Sikhs,* New Delhi, 1983.
- Hodson, H.V. : *The Great Divide,* London, 1969.
- Husain, Azim : *Fazal-I-Husain : A Political Biography,* Bombay; 1946.
- Johnson, Campbell : *A Mission with Mountbatten,* London, 1951.
- Jones, Keneth W. : *Arya Dharam-Hindu Consciousness in the Nineteenth Century in Punjab,* Delhi, 1976.
- Kushwant Singh : *A History of the Sikhs, (1839—1974),* Vol. II, Delhi, 1966.
- Kirpal Singh : *The Partition of Punjab,* Patiala, 1971.
- Kshtish : *Storm in Punjab,* New Delhi, 1985.

- Kumar, Ravinder : *Essay in the Social History of Modern India,* Delhi, 1963.
- Lal, K. Sajan : *A Short History of Urdu Newspapers,* Hyderabad, 1964.
- Lamba, Krishan Gopal : *Dynamics of Punjabi Suba Movement,* New Delhi, 1999.
- Landas, Stephen P. : *The Exchange of Minorities,* New York, 1932.
- Majumdar, R.C. : *History of the Freedom Movement in India,* Vol. III, Calcutta, 1963.
- Malhotra, S.L. : *Gandhi and the Punjab,* Chandigarh, 1970.
- Malhotra, V.P. : *Economic Condition of Displaced Persons Settled in East Punjab,* Vol. I, Ludhiana, 1949.
- Mathur, Y.B. : *Quit India Movement,* Delhi, 1979.
- Menon, V.P. : *The Story of the Integration of Indian States,* Bombay, 1956.
- Menon, V.P. : *Transfer of Power in India,* Princeton, 1957.
- Misra, B.B. : *The Indian Middle Classes,* New Delhi, 1978.
- Mittal, S.C. : *Freedom Movement in Punjab, 1905—29,* New Delhi, 1977.
- Mohan Lal : *Disintegration of Punjab,* Chandigarh, 1984.
- Moon, Penderal : *Divide and Quit,* London, 1961
- Nagar, Purushotam : *Lala Lajpat Rai,* Delhi, 1977.
- Nagarkar, V.V. : *Genesis of Pakistan,* New Delhi, 1975.
- Nair, L.R. (ed.) : *Rural Rehabilitation in East Punjab, 1947-48,* Shimla, 1948.
- Nair, L.R. (ed.) : *Sikander Hyat Khan : The Soldier Statesman of the Punjab,* Lahore, 1943.
- Nanda, B.R. : *Mahatma Gandhi : A Biography,* London, 1958.
- Nanda, J. : *Punjab Uprooted,* Bombay, 1948.
- Narain, Iqbal (ed.) : *State Politics in National Perspective,* New Delhi, 1986.

- Narang, A.S. : *Storm Over the Sutlej—The Akali Politics,* New Delhi, 1983.
- Narang, G.C. : *Glorious Hinduism,* New Delhi, 1966.
- Nayar, B.R. : *Minority Politics in the Punjab,* Princeton, 1966.
- Nehru, Jawaharlal : *Autobiography,* Bombay, 1952.
- Nidharak, Teja Singh : *Mockery with Democracy,* Shimla, 1948.
- Pandey, Dhanpatti : *The Arya Samaj and Indian Nationalism,* New Delhi, 1972.
- Pannikar, K.M. : *A Survey of Indian History,* Bombay, 1974.
- Pyare Lal : *Mahatma Gandhi-The Last Phase,* Vol. II, Ahmedabad, 1958.
- Pylee, M.V. : *Constitutional History of India, 1600-1950,* Bombay, 1950.
- Rai, Gulshan : *Formation of Haryana,* Delhi, 1987.
- Rai, Satya M. : *Legislative Politics and the Freedom Struggle in the Punjab, 1897—1947,* New Delhi, 1987.
- Rai, Satya M. : *Partition of Punjab,* New Delhi, 1963.
- Rai, Satya M. : *Punjab Heroic Tradition,* Patiala, 1975.
- Rai, Satya M. : *Punjab Since Partition,* Delhi, 1986.
- Rajinder Kaur : *Sikh Identity and National integration,* New Delhi, 1992.
- Ram, Raja : *The Jallianwala Bagh Massacre,* Chandigarh, 1969.
- Randhawa, M.S. : *Out of Ashes,* Bombay, 1954.
- Rao, M.V. Ramana : *A Short History of the Indian National Congress,* Delhi, 1959.
- Sandhu, Devinder Pal : *Sikhs in Indian Politics : Study of a Minority,* New Delhi, 1992.
- Sarhadi, A.S. : *Punjabi Suba : The Story of Struggle,* Delhi, 1970.

- Sharma, Kamlesh : *Role of Muslims in Indian Politics, 1857—1947,* New Delhi, 1985.
- Sitaramayya, P. : *History of the Indian National Congress,* Delhi, 1969.
- Tuker, F. : *While Memory Serves,* London, 1950.
- Tuteja, K.L. : *Sikh Politics (1920—40),* Kurukshetra, 1989.
- Verma, Manju : *The Coalition Ministries in Punjab,* Patiala, 1978.
- Wadhwa, Kamlesh Kumar : *Minority Safeguards in India,* Faridabad, 1975.
- Walia, Ramesh : *Praja Mandal Movement in East Punjab States,* Patiala, 1972.
- Wallace, Paul and Surendra Chopra : *Political Dynamics of Punjab,* Amritsar, 1981.
- Weiner, Myren (ed.) : *State Politics in India,* Princeton, 1968.
- Weiner, Myren and John Osgood Field : *Electrol Politics in the Indian States : Party Systems and Cleavages,* Delhi, 1975.
- West, Geoffery : *Line of Annie Besant,* London, 1929.
- Yadav, K.C. : *Builders of Our Nation—Murlidhar,* Kurukshetra, 1987.
- Yadav, K.C. : *Punjab Elections, 1920—47,* Tokyo, 1981.

Books in Punjabi

- Arora, A.C. : *Punjab Dian Lok Lehran, 1847—1947,* Patiala, 1989.
- Dard, Hira Singh : *Panth : Dharam Te Rajniti,* Jullundhar, n.d.
- Dilgeer, Harinder Singh : *Shiromani Akali Dal : Ik Itihas,* Jullundhar, 1970.
- Fateh Singh : *Abhul Yaadan,* Ganganagar, 1962.
- Jaswant Singh (ed.) : *Master Tara Singh : Jiwan Sangarsh Te Udesh,* Amritsar, 1972.

- Master Tara Singh : *Meri Yaad,* Amritsar, 1945.

Book In Urdu

- Hamdard, Sadhu Singh : *Azad Punjab,* Amritsar, 1943.

Unpublished Ph.D. Thesis

- Pardaman Singh : *The Administration of India Under Lord Minto, 1905—10,* Chandigarh, 1976.
- Parmar, Surinder Singh : *History of Bhartiya Jan Sangh in Punjab,* Chandigarh, 1987.

Index

H

I

J

K

L

M

N